A LEGAL FRAMEWORK FOR SECURITY IN EUROPEAN HEALTH CARE TELEMATICS

Studies in Health Technology and Informatics

Editors

Volume 74

Previously published in this series

Vol. 45. J. Dudeck, B. Blobel, W. Lordieck and T. Bürkle (Eds.), New Technologies in Hospital Information Systems
Vol. 46. U. Gerdin, M. Tallberg and P. Wainwright (Eds.), Nursing Informatics
Vol. 47. W. Ceusters, P. Spyns, G. De Moor and W. Martin (Eds.), Syntactic-Semantic Tagging of Medical Texts: The Multi-TALE Project
Vol. 48. J. Graafmans, V. Taipale and N. Charness (Eds.), Gerontechnology
Vol. 49. L. van den Broek and A.J. Sikkel (Eds.), Health Cards '97
Vol. 50. J.D. Westwood, H.M. Hoffman, D. Stredney and S.J. Weghorst (Eds.), Medicine Meets Virtual Reality
Vol. 51. J. Mantas (Ed.), Advances in Health Telematics Education
Vol. 52. B. Cesnik, A.T. McCray and J.-R. Scherrer (Eds.), MedInfo '98
Vol. 53. M.C. Sievert, D.E. Moxley, N.J. Ogg and T.B. Patrick, Thesaurus of Health Informatics
Vol. 54. O. Ferrer-Roca and M. Sosa-Iudicissa (Eds.), Handbook of Telemedicine
Vol. 55. H.M.J. Goldschmidt, M.J.T. Cox, R.J.E. Grouls, W.A.J.H. van de Laar and G.G. van Merode, Reference Information Model for Clinical Laboratories
Vol. 56. I. Iakovidis, S. Maglavera and A. Trakatellis (Eds.), User Acceptance of Health Telematics Applications
Vol. 57. J. Mantas (Ed.), Health and Medical Informatics Education in Europe
Vol. 58. G. Riva, B.K. Wiederhold and E. Molinari (Eds.), Virtual Environments in Clinical Psychology and Neuroscience
Vol. 59. I.A.F. Stokes (Ed.), Research into Spinal Deformities 2
Vol. 60. M. Di Rienzo, G. Mancia, G. Parati, A. Pedotti and A. Zanchetti (Eds.), Methodology and Clinical Applications of Blood Pressure and Heart Rate Analysis
Vol. 61. R.A. Mortensen (Ed.), ICNP® and Telematic Applications for Nurses in Europe
Vol. 62. J.D. Westwood, H.M. Hoffman, R.A. Robb and D. Stredney (Eds.), Medicine Meets Virtual Reality
Vol. 63. R. Rogers and J. Reardon, Recommendations for International Action
Vol. 64. M. Nerlich and R. Kretschmer (Eds.), The Impact of Telemedicine on Health Care Management
Vol. 65. In production
Vol. 66. In production
Vol. 67. J. Oates and H. Bjerregaard Jensen (Eds.), Building Regional Health Care Networks in Europe
Vol. 68. P. Kokol, B. Zupan, J. Stare, M. Premik and R. Engelbrecht (Eds.), Medical Informatics Europe '99
Vol. 69. In production
Vol. 70. J.D. Westwood, H.M. Hoffman, G.T. Mogel, R.A. Robb and D. Stredney (Eds.), Medicine Meets Virtual Reality 2000
Vol. 71. J.T. Ottesen and M. Danielsen (Eds.), Mathematical Modelling in Medicine
Vol. 72. I. Iakovidis, S. Maglavera and A. Trakatellis (Eds.), User Acceptance of Health Telematics Applications
Vol. 73. W. Sermeus, N. Kearney, J. Kinnunen, L. Goossens, M. Miller (Eds.), WISECARE.

ISSN: 0926-9630

A Legal Framework for Security in European Health Care Telematics

Edited by

Otto Rienhoff

Department of Medical Informatics, University of Göttingen, Germany

Caroline Laske

International Legal Consultant, Brussels, Belgium

Patrick van Eecke

Interdisciplinary Centre for Law and Information Technology, Leuven, Belgium

Paul Wenzlaff

Physicians Chamber of Lower Saxony, Hannover, Germany

and

Ursula Piccolo

Department of Medical Informatics, University of Göttingen, Germany

IOS Press

Ohmsha

Amsterdam • Berlin • Oxford • Tokyo • Washington, DC

ISBN 1 58603 049 3 (IOS Press)
ISBN 4 274 90397 4 C3047 (Ohmsha)
Library of Congress Catalog Card Number: 00-106863

Publisher
IOS Press
Nieuwe Hemweg 6B
1013 BG Amsterdam
The Netherlands
fax: +31 20 620 3419
e-mail: order@iospress.nl

Distributor in the UK and Ireland
IOS Press/Lavis Marketing
73 Lime Walk
Headington
Oxford OX3 7AD
England
fax: +44 1865 75 0079

Distributor in the USA and Canada
IOS Press, Inc.
5795-G Burke Centre Parkway
Burke, VA 22015
USA
fax: +1 703 323 3668
e-mail: iosbooks@iospress.com

Distributor in Germany
IOS Press
Spandauer Strasse 2
D-10178 Berlin
Germany
fax: +49 30 242 3113

Distributor in Japan
Ohmsha, Ltd.
3-1 Kanda Nishiki-cho
Chiyoda-ku, Tokyo 101
Japan
fax: +81 3 3233 2426

PRINTED IN THE NETHERLANDS

Main Partners

Spri, Swedish Institute for Health Services Development
PCLS, Physicians Chamber of Lower Saxony

Preface

The importance of health care is obvious, and so are the advantages that information and communication technology is bringing to health care, its quality, its availability and its affordability. Equally important, however, is security. Security for health care information systems is not only a technical matter, it is a social goal to be achieved and to be maintained by acknowledging the social values in which such systems operate, such as the essential relationship of trust between the patient and the doctor and individual as well collective privacy, values which find their expression in the normative environment of these systems. As the report shows observing security from this perspective, in time, turns legal requirements from obstacles to assets for successful implementation and acceptance.

The report is the result of a collaborative European effort; collaborative across national and linguistic boundaries, collaborative as regards the disciplines involved in its production, and collaborative as it concerns the various sub-disciplines of law dealing with these issues. With this broad approach the report represents another essential element for the future of health care information systems in our societies: Health care information systems will reflect the increasing mobility of the European citizens, the diversity of the services they will expect within Europe, the information and communication needs these services will produce and the complex legal environment in which they have to operate.

As recently shown by the European Directive on data protection and by the efforts of establishing a European sytem of secure transactions, in this context too, the legal environment ist the expression of common expectations as regards the values to be observed in the European information and communication society.

The report addresses these issues in a clear language bridging the disciplines, providing highly useful policy tools for project leaders and for decision makers in the Health Telematics field.

Prof. Dr. Herbert Burkert
University of St. Gallen
Chairman, Legal Advisory Board for the Information Market
To DG XIII of the European Commission

Preface

For several year the Physicians Chamber of Lower Saxony (PCLS) has supported the development of secure communication networks in health care. Results of the participation in the European projects TrustHealth 1, SIREN, and G7-Health Data Cards as well as from several national activities like the Arbeitskreis Health Professional Card are condensed into this book. The fruitful collaboration between PCLS and Professor Rienhoff who headed the "legal workpackage" of the SIREN project started in 1980 when Rienhoff became the first "data-protection-officer" of the Kassenärztliche Vereinigung Niedersachsen. Already in the seventies phrasing and implementation of the data protection laws took place in a close cooperation between Professor Kilian from the University of Hannover and the late Professor Reichertz from Hannover Medical School, academic teacher of the three German authors of this book.

The collaboration with C. Laske and P. van Eecke is more recent but became a cornerstone in our activities: both of them being at home in several European legal cultures and outstanding experts in their fields.

During the next decade IT-systems will change drastically the way health care systems are operating. Quality management, continous medical education, new patient services, knowledge management, bioinformatics, microtechnology and tele-services will change the way how physicians help their patients. However, if patients and doctors shall trust these new powerful tools security and dataprotection have to be guaranteed. The Physicians Chamber of Lower Saxony will therefore continue to support all intellectual, organisational, legal, and technical developments which together may assemble the guarantee needed.

Prof. Dr. Heyo Eckel
President, Physicians Chamber of Lower Saxony
President, German Senat for Continuous Medical Education

Table of Contents

Executive Summary

Framework

The aim of this report is to examine how questions of law currently impact on the development of Health Telematics. It is based on an intense dialogue between many legal and telematics experts as well as Health Telematics policy makers and leaders of Health Telematics projects.

On the global scale it could be demonstrated by the so-called G-7/8 projects how efficiently Health Telematics can support various functions in public health and health care. However, since the 1970s data protection issues have been addressed as possible obstacles to the extensive use of information technology (IT) in health care. The European Health Telematics projects of the IVth and Vth Framework Programme as well as international experience suggest that in the current debate about telemedicine and global networking liability aspects have become the main issue of concern.

This report has been written as a practical tool for those working in the management of health care and Health Telematics. It provides quick and easy reference to relevant legal issues in the context of a given or planned project. To keep the report short and focussed, only the most important examples of IT use in Health Telematics are examined.

The report is structured into eight sections: Section 1 describes the report's underlying boundaries and principal assumptions. This section also analyses the current legal situation. Section 2 describes the methodology used to analyse liability aspects of telemedicine and how to draw up a legal reference model. Section 3 describes the relevant liability issues in relation to two telemedicine scenarios, and briefly examines the legal situation in various European countries. The fourth section describes how technical developments in Health Telematics are dealt with in new laws and regulations and how, from an understanding of this long-term process, one can derive helpful steps to develop early solutions for difficult legal problems. Section 5 addresses specific issues in Health Telematics like imaging, medical research or registries. Section 6 summerises recommendations for future work. Section 7 formulates an outlook on the European scene. Section 8 contains the documents of several legal workshops and lists other relevant documents and institutions. An index of names and subjects supports the reader in finding relevant paragraphs of the report.

Readers with little time who wish to focus on the telemedicine problem analysis can immediately go to Section 3 provided he/she has some basic knowledge of the legal problems in the field. Colleagues looking for an introductory approach should follow the sequence of the current report. The senior health professional looking for systematisation in the question will certainly interpret the contents of Section 4 for his/her own legal environment. If you wish to use the book as a reference, just study the executive summary, the chapter headings and the available indexes of literature and list of laws and regulations.

Results

This report examines the current legal issues in the field of telemedicine and telematics in health to support politicians, health managers, and project leaders in Health Telematics. It links topical questions of liability, intellectual property rights, and data protection to European legislative actions, directives, and to national law of the European Member States. Taking into account the underlying historical and cultural aspects, the report is based on extensive interviewing and workshop discussions with experts of health ministries, insurance companies, professional organisations etc., as well as on academic analysis. The main results of this book stem from the Legal Workpackage in the European Accompanying Measure SIREN ("Security in Regional Networks"), contracted to the Physicians Chamber of Lower Saxony, Germany.

The report was written and edited by a group of German and Belgian experts who have been working in the field for many years. The interdisciplinary group comprised technical security experts, legal experts, and medical data protection experts who came from three different backgrounds: physicians chamber, international legal consultancies, and academia.

It was also possible to take into account other recent material from various studies which were not a part of the SIREN Accompanying Measure, but which related directly to this issue, such as the G-7/8 studies "Enabling Mechanisms" and "Health Data Cards", from an extensive study for DG XV regarding digital signatures in Europe, the EU projects SEISMED/ISHTAR and TrustHealth 1, and everyday legal work in several international consultancies.

The study found that liability issues are a major obstacle to increase the use of Health Telematics and telemedicine. The liability question is analysed using two rather simple, but currently relevant case examples:

- international teleconsultation on a given case, and
- international exchange of patient data in cases of medical emergencies.

These examples are illustrated in relation to seven liability concepts which are formulated and discussed in an interdisciplinary approach. For each concept it is described whether digital signature and encryption can improve the legal situation.

It is found that in most instances, the availability of digital signatures and trusted third party schemes as well as cryptography considerably improves the legal situation in Health Telematics. However, when the study examined the current status of legal developments in different European countries and on the European level in general and in relation to Health Telematics, technologies such as digital signatures, trusted third party schemes, and cryptography were found to evolve only recently. Further developments in Health Telematics and telemedicine cannot prosper on a broad basis without security structures. Immediate and strategic action is therefore essential.

Two legal workshops held in late 1996 and autumn 1998 proved that neither legal academics nor health policy makers were sufficiently aware of how relevant it is to develop and implement legal solutions in everyday Health Telematics practice. In many national ministries of health the issue was considered to be of a general nature that should be dealt with by the Ministry of Justice or Ministry of Interior. This report, however, emphasises the fact that the cultural traditions in most of the European Member States have fostered the growth of a diversity of legal regulations for the Health Telematics field. It is hence only theoretically possible to expect appropriate general solutions for the typical liability questions that exist in the field of Health Telematics.

The report, therefore, recommends to project leaders to consider seriously the issue in their proposals and projects, as legal aspects may become the key obstacles to general acceptance of telematic systems in Health Telematics. It recommends to policy makers in health to address the matter and to analyse how national regulations have to be adapted to allow for digital signature schemes, trusted third parties, and encryption in Health Telematics and telemedicine. And it recommends to legal experts to formulate model contracts between parties prepared to offer teleconsultancy or to send data to treating professionals based on or referring to professional Codes of Good Practice. This systematic approach could be a key element in the development of Health Telematics systems in coming years, before clearer and stricter general legal regulations have been issued and adopted in Europe and in the European Member States.

Finally, the report analyses how the development of Health Telematics is dynamically mapped into the adoption or creation of legal constructs which regulate Health Telematics in society. It becomes clear from this formal approach that a few laws or regulations will not fundamentally clarify the issue. Instead, legal adjustments must aim to keep up with the continuous technical developments. The fact that the development cycles in law are considerably longer than in the technological field leaves controversial gaps and uncertainties.

General Recommendations for Future Work in the EU

The description of the most important aspects of this report allows to derive some general recommendations for future work regarding legal aspects of Health Telematics for the European Commission abstracting from the more detailed recommendations of the second legal workshop as documented on page 145/6/7:

1. In view of the compexity of the issue considerable time will be necessary to harmonize national legal regulations and international professional agreements. Private law solutions can be first step solutions.
   In the meantime the development of European or global codes of good practice and ethics is urgently necessary to support the development of national and especially cross border health telematic systems.
2. A set of model-contracts which can be used between patients and service providers or between different service providers in the field of tele-consultancy is urgently needed. They shall cover the most common solutions which can be expected in telemedicine within the next two to three years.
3. A strong collaboration between health professional societies in the European Union is of vital interest to start harmonisation of professional regulation and specifically of authentication procedures in the different member countries. In addition, a harmonisation of the professional registration procedures would be extremely helpful as they would be the basis for smooth operation of trusted third parties' services.
4. Research into the new legal issues raised by the future developments in medicine and Health Telematics technology is urgently required, specifically in relation to the consequences of molecular medicine, genome analyses, and virtual reality systems.
5. The complexity of the issues is as impressive as the scarcity of senior professionals in the field who are able to integrate knowledge about Health Telematics, law and medicine. This defies that plain solutions put forward by individual technically oriented projects will gain any general momentum. The supplementation of curricula regarding this issue is urgently necessary.
6. As many overseas countries are interested in tele-collaboration with European institutions in health care and as international tele-consulting may become reality in a few years, all European projects should address the legal matter following developments in the so-called G-7/8 projects and should contain corresponding training modules for the end users.
7. In addition to all protective action and infrastructure like digital signatures and encryption the legal systems need to address measures against criminal action in networks, to prevent programming, distribution and execution of destructive software or intrusion into private sphere.

Zusammenfassung

Rahmen

Es ist das Ziel dieses Berichtes, den gegenwärtigen Einfluß rechtlicher Regelungen auf die Entwicklung von Telematik im Gesundheitswesen zu analysieren. Er wurde auf der Basis eines intensiven Dialoges mit vielen Experten aus den juristischen und telematischen Disziplinen sowie Gesundheitspolitikern und Leitern von Projekten im Bereich Gesundheitstelematik erstellt.

Durch die sogenannten G-7/8 Projekte konnte im globalen Maßstab gezeigt werden, wie effizient Gesundheitstelematik diverse Funktionen im Gesundheitswesen unterstützen kann. Seit den 70iger Jahren werden jedoch Fragen des Datenschutzes im Lichte eines möglichen Mißbrauchs der Informationstechnologien (IT) im Gesundheitssektor diskutiert. Die Ergebnisse der europäischen Gesundheitstelematikprojekte des IV. und V. Rahmenprogramms lassen ebenso wie internationale Erfahrungen in diesem Sektor vermuten, dass Aspekte der Haftung zum Hauptthema der laufenden Debatte über Telemedizin und die globale Vernetzung im Gesundheitswesen werden.

Dieser Bericht ist als praktische Hilfe für all jene gedacht, die leitend im Gesundheitswesen und in der Gesundheitstelematik arbeiten. Er hilft dem Leser, im Rahmen eines gegebenen oder geplanten Projektes schnell zu den relevanten juristischen Punkten zu finden. Um den Report konzentriert und prägnant zu halten, wurden hier nur die wichtigsten Beispiele der IT-Nutzung im Gesundheitssektor angeführt.

Der Bericht gliedert sich in acht Kapitel: Kapitel 1 beschreibt die Annahmen und inherenten Grenzen, die dem Bericht zu Grunde liegen. Es analysiert ferner die gegenwärtige Gesetzeslage. Kapitel 2 beschreibt die angewandte Methodologie, mit der Haftungsaspekte im Bereich Telemedizin analysiert wurden und ein rechtsbezogenes Referenzmodell abgeleitet wurde. Kapitel 3 stellt die relevanten Haftungsfragen in Bezug auf zwei telemedizinische Szenarien dar und beleuchtet kurz die Rechtssituation in verschiedenen europäischen Ländern. Das vierte Kapitel beschreibt, wie technische Entwicklungen im Bereich Gesundheitstelematik in neue gesetzliche Regelungen eingebunden werden und wie man hilfreiche Schritte zur frühzeitigen Lösung schwieriger rechtlicher Probleme aus dem Verständnis dieses langfristigen Prozesses ableiten kann. Kapitel 5 befaßt sich mit spezifischen Themen von Gesundheitstelematik, wie bildgebende Verfahren, klinische Forschung oder Fallregister. Kapitel 6 faßt Empfehlungen für die zukünftige Arbeit zusammen. Kapitel 7 formuliert einen Ausblick auf die europäische Szene. Kapitel 8 beinhaltet die Dokumentation diverser juristischer Workshops und führt weitere relevante Dokumente und Institutionen auf. Ein Namens- und Schlagwörterverzeichnis ermöglicht es dem Leser, rasch für ihn besonders relevante Abschnitte des Berichtes zu finden.

Eilige Leser, die sich in erster Linie auf die Analyse der Telemedizinproblematik konzentrieren möchten, können direkt zu Kapitel 3 springen, sofern sie in etwa mit den juristischen Fragen dieses Bereiches vertraut sind. Kollegen, die eher eine Einführung in den Themenkomplex suchen, sollten in ihrer Lektüre der vorgegebenen Gliederung des Berichtes folgen. Erfahrene Berufstätige im Gesundheitswesen, die an einer Systematisierung der Fragestellung interessiert sind, werden gewiß den Inhalt des Kapitels 4 für die eigene Situation auslegen. Falls das Buch zum Nachschlagen genutzt werden soll, empfiehlt sich einfach die Lektüre der Zusammenfassung, der Kapitelüberschriften, der angebotenen Indizes sowie der Literaturlisten und Listen von gesetzlichen Verordnungen.

Ergebnisse

Dieser Bericht untersucht die aktuellen juristischen Themen im Bereich der Telemedizin und der Telematik im Gesundheitswesen. Damit will er Politikern, Gesundheitmanagern und Projektleitern im Bereich Gesundheitstelematik eine Hilfestellung geben. Der Bericht verbindet dabei die gegenwärtig so dringlichen Fragen der Haftung, des Rechtes an geistigem Eigentum und des Datenschutzes mit der Entwicklung europäischer Direktiven, Empfehlungen und Rechtsvorhaben sowie dem nationalen Recht in den europäischen Mitgliedstaaten. Der Bericht basiert auf umfangreichen Interviews und Workshops mit Experten aus den Gesundheitsministerien, aus Versicherungsgesellschaften, Berufsorganisationen, etc. einerseits sowie auf akademischen Analysen andererseits und trägt dabei auch historischen und kulturellen Aspekten Rechnung. Die Hauptergebnisse dieses Buches leiten sich aus dem Arbeitspaket "Rechtliche Aspekte" der europäischen Begleitmaßnahme SIREN („Security in Regional Networks" - Sicherheit in Regionalen Netzen) ab. Dieses Arbeitspaket wurde vertraglich an die Ärztekammer Niedersachsen vergeben.

Verfasst und editiert wurde der Bericht von einer deutsch-belgischen Expertengruppe, deren Mitglieder seit Jahren in diesem Bereich tätig sind. Experten für technische Sicherheit, für das Rechtswesen und den gesetzlichen Datenschutz in der Medizin bildeten diese interdisziplinäre Gruppe, deren Mitglieder drei professionellenWurzeln entstammen: Ärztekammer, internationales juristisches Consulting und Wissenschaft.

Auch aktuelle Materialien, die nicht aus der SIREN-Begleitmaßnahme stammten, sondern aus anderen, jedoch in direktem thematischen Zusammenhang stehenden Projekten, konnten einbezogen werden: Zu nennen sind hier insbesondere die G-7/8 Studien „Enabling Mechanisms" und „Health Data Cards" sowie eine im Auftrag der Europäischen Kommission (DG XV) durchgeführte umfassende Studie zur Frage der digitalen Unterschrift in Europa. Zudem wurden Materialien aus den EU-Projekten SEISMED/ISHTAR und TrustHealth 1 ebenso berücksichtigt wie die Alltagserfahrungen mehrerer internationaler juristischer Beratungsgesellschaften.

Die Studie ergab, dass Haftungsprobleme ein Haupthindernis für die zunehmende Nutzung von Gesundheitstelematik und Telemedizin darstellen. Die Haftungsfrage wird anhand zweier einfacher, aber aktuell relevanter Fallbeispiele erläutert:

- internationale Telekonsultation zu einem gegebenen Fall und
- internationaler Austausch von Patientendaten in medizinischen Notfällen.

Diese Beispiele werden im Hinblick auf sieben Haftungskonzepte von einer interdisziplinären Warte aus erörtert. Für jedes Konzept wird beschrieben, ob digitale Signatur und Verschlüsselung die rechtliche Situation verbessern können.

In der Mehrheit der Fälle ergibt sich eine beträchtliche Verbesserung der juristischen Situation im Bereich der Gesundheitstelematik, sobald digitale Unterschriften, eine organisatorische Sicherheitsinfrastruktur mit Vertrauensstellen (Trusted Third Party - TTP) und Kryptographie zur Verfügung stehen. Eine Untersuchung im Rahmen der Studie bezüglich des derzeitigen Standes rechtlicher Entwicklungen in verschiedenen europäischen Ländern sowie der europäischen Rechtsprechung im Allgemeinen zeigte jedoch, dass Konzepte für digitale Signaturen, TTP-Dienste und Kryptographie erst in den Anfängen begriffen sind. Die weitere Entwicklung von Telematik und Telemedizin kann ohne solche Sicherheitsstrukturen nicht auf breiter Basis fortschreiten. Sofortiges und strategisches Handeln ist daher unabdingbar.

Zwei Ende 1996 und im Herbst 1998 durchgeführte Workshops zeigten, dass weder Akademikern im Bereich der Rechtswissenschaften noch Gesundheitspolitikern ausreichend bewußt ist, wie wichtig die Entwicklung und Umsetzung gesetzlicher Lösungen für die alltägliche Praxis im Gesundheitswesen sind. Von vielen nationalen Gesundheitsministerien wurde das Problem als von generellem Belang eingestuft, für das nicht sie, sondern die Justiz- oder Innenministerien zuständig wären. Dieser Bericht betont demgegenüber, dass die kulturellen Traditionen in den meisten europäischen Mitgliedsstaaten die Ausbildung unterschiedlicher gesetzlicher Regelungen für das Gesundheitswesens gefördert haben. Es wäre von daher nur theoretisch möglich, geeignete allgemeine Lösungsansätze für die typischen Haftungsfragen im Bereich des Gesundheitswesens zu erwarten.

Die Empfehlung dieses Berichtes an Projektleiter lautet deshalb, den Gegenstand ernsthaft in ihren Vorschlägen und Projekten zu berücksichtigen, da in Zukunft gerade juristische Aspekte einer generellen Akzeptanz von Telematiksystemen in der Gesundheitstelematik entgegenstehen könnten. Die Empfehlung an Gesundheitspolitiker geht dahin, sich des Themas anzunehmen und zu analysieren, wie nationale Verordnungen angepaßt werden müßten, um den Einsatz von digitalen Signaturen, Verschlüsselungs-techniken und TTP-Diensten im Bereich Telematik im Gesundheitswesen und in der

Telemedizin zu ermöglichen. Die Empfehlung an juristische Experten schließlich lautet, Modelverträge zwischen Parteien, die Telekonsultation anbieten wollen oder die Daten an behandelnde Ärzte schicken möchten, zu formulieren, und zwar auf der Basis eines oder in Bezug auf einen *Code of Good Practice*. Dieser systematische Ansatz könnte ein Schlüsselelement für die Entwicklung von Gesundheitstelematiksystemen in den kommenden Jahren sein, bis klarere und strengere allgemeine gesetzliche Regelungen formuliert und in Europa und den europäischen Mitgliedsstaaten etabliert sind.

Schließlich analysiert der Bericht, wie die Entwicklung von Gesundheitstelematik dynamisch auf die Annahme oder Errichtung rechtlicher Konstrukte zur Regulierung der Gesundheitstelematik in der Gesellschaft abgebildet wird. Aus diesem formalen Ansatz wird klar, daß von einigen wenigen Gesetzen oder Verordnungen keine prinzipielle Klärung des Themas zu erwarten ist. Vielmehr muß die gesetzliche Anpassung sich bemühen, mit der kontinuierlichen technischen Entwicklung Schritt zu halten. Die Tatsache, dass die legislativen Zyklen deutlich länger sind als die der technischen Entwicklung eröffnet dabei Kontroversen, Lücken und Unsicherheiten.

Allgemeine Empfehlungen für die zukünftige Arbeit in der EU

Die Beschreibung der wichtigsten Aspekte dieses Berichtes erlaubt es, einige allgemeine Empfehlungen für die zukünftige Arbeit im Hinblick auf die juristischen Aspekte von Telematik im Gesundheitswesen für die Europäische Kommission abzuleiten, indem man von den detaillierteren Empfehlungen des Zweiten Workshops (wie auf den Seiten 145/6/7 dokumentiert) abstrahiert:

1. Angesichts der Komplexität der in Frage stehenden Probleme wird erheblicher Zeitbedarf zu veranschlagen sein, um die nationalen gesetzlichen Regelungen und die internationalen Übereinkommen im Bereich der Gesundheitsberufe zu harmonisieren. Regelungen innerhalb des privaten Sektors ermöglichen erste Schritte zur Lösung dieser Problematik. In der Zwischenzeit ist die Entwicklung eines europäischen oder globalen Verhaltens-Codex sowie einer entsprechenden Ethik dringend geboten, um die Entwicklung von nationalen und insbesondere supranationalen Telematiksystemen im Gesundheitswesen zu unterstützen.
2. Dringend benötigt werden Musterverträge, die zwischen Patienten und Dienstleistenden oder zwischen verschiedenen dienstleistenden Parteien im Bereich der Telekonsultation eingesetzt werden können. Diese sollten die häufigsten Fälle abdecken, die voraussichtlich in den nächsten zwei oder drei Jahren in der Telemedizin auftreten werden.
3. Eine enge Zusammenarbeit zwischen den Berufsverbänden des Gesundheitssektors innerhalb der Europäischen Union ist für den Beginn der Harmonisierung der

gesetzlichen Verordnungen und speziell der Authentifizierungsprozesse in den verschiedenen Mitgliedsländern von vitalem Interesse. Zudem wäre eine Harmonisierung der Approbationsmodi extrem hilfreich, da diese die Basis für ein reibungsloses Funktionieren von TTP-Diensten bilden.

4. Die neuen gesetzlichen Fragestellungen, die sich durch zukünftige Entwicklungen in der Medizin- und Gesundheitstelematik ergeben, müssen dringend erforscht werden, insbesondere bezüglich der Konsequenzen von Molekularmedizin, Genom Analysen und Virtual Reality Systemen.
5. Die Komplexität der Fragestellungen ist im gleichen Maße beeindruckend wie die Seltenheit von führenden Fachpersonen in diesem Bereich, die gleichermassen in Gesundheitstelematik, Rechtswerken und Medizin ausgewiesen sind. Diese Tatsache spricht dagegen, daß „einfache" Lösungen, wie sie von vielen verschiedenen, rein technisch orientierten Projekten vorgeschlagen werden, sich in irgendeiner Weise allgemein auswirken werden. Die Ergänzung der Curricula mit dieser Thematik ist dringend geboten.
6. Da viele Länder in Übersee an einer telematischen Zusammenarbeit mit europäischen Institutionen des Gesundheitswesens interessiert sind und da internationale Telekonsultationen auf globaler Ebene in wenigen Jahren Realität sein könnten, sollten alle europäischen Projekte das Problem angehen. Die Projekte sollten darin Entwicklungen in den sogenannten G-7/8 Projekten folgen und entsprechende Trainingsmodule in ihre Programme für die Anwender aufnehmen.
7. Zusätzlich zu allen Schutzmaßnahmen und zu Infrastrukturen wie Digitale Unterschrift und Verschlüsselung müssen die juristischen Systeme Maßnahmen in Angriff nehmen gegen kriminelle Akte in Netzen, wie die Programmierung, Verteilung und Ausführung von destruktiver Software oder das Einbrechen in die Privatsphäre.

Résumé

Cadre général

Le but de ce rapport est de faire le point sur l'incidence des problèmes juridiques sur le développement de la télématique dans le domaine de la santé. Il est le résultat de discussions intenses entre un grand nombre d'experts des disciplines juridique et télématique, des hommes politiques du secteur santé ainsi que des promoteurs de projets télématiques dans le domaine de la santé.

D'une manière générale, on a pu démontrer dans le cadre des projets dits G7/G8 que la télématique peut, d'une manière efficace, soutenir diverses fonctions dans le secteur de la santé. Cependant, depuis les années 1970, il y a une tendance à voir les problèmes de protection des données sensibles comme des obstacles potentiels à une utilisation intensive des techniques de l'informatique (IT) dans la santé publique. Les projets de télématique européens des Quatrième et Cinquième programme cadres ainsi que l'expérience internationale conduisent à penser que les aspects de responsabilité juridique sont devenus le sujet principal de discussion concernant la télémédecine et la mise en réseau global .

Ce rapport fut conçu comme un outil pratique pour ceux qui travaillent dans la gestion des systèmes de soin et la télématique. Il offre un accès rapide et facile aux questions juridiques qui se posent dans le contexte d'un projet existant ou futur. Dans le but de rendre le rapport concis, les auteurs se sont concentrés sur les exemples les plus importants de l'emploi des technologies de l'information dans la santé.

Le rapport est divisé en huit sections: La première décrit le cadre et les hypothèses principales du rapport. Elle analyse aussi la situation juridique actuelle. La deuxième section décrit la méthodologie utilisée pour analyser les aspects de responsabilité juridique dans l'exercice de la télémédecine et sur la manière d'établir un modèle juridique de référence. La troisième décrit les questions de responsabilité vues en relation de deux cas de télémédecine et examine brièvement la situation dans plusieurs pays européens. La quatrième section décrit comment les développements techniques en télématique sont pris en compte dans les nouvelles lois et réglementations et comment, en comprenant bien ce long processus, il est possible de prendre des dispositions pour développer des solutions très tôt pour des problèmes juridiques difficiles.

La cinquième section est consacrée aux aspects spécifiques de certains domaines de télématique de santé, comme l'imagerie, la recherche médicale ou les registres. La sixième section résume les recommandations pour le travail futur. La septième section présente une vision de la situation en Europe. La huitième section contient les documents de plusieurs sessions de travail juridiques et donne la liste d'autres documents et institutions utiles. Un index des noms et des sujets traités aide le lecteur à trouver les paragraphes correspondant du rapport.

Les lecteurs pressés qui désirent se concentrer sur l'analyse des problèmes de télémédecine peuvent aller directement à la troisième section, pourvu qu'il/ qu'elle soit un peu familier avec les questions juridiques du domaine. Aux collègues cherchant une approche plus progressive, il est par contre recommandé de suivre la séquence du rapport. Le professionnel de santé expérimenté à la recherche d'une systématisation de la question va certainement interpréter le contenu de la quatrième partie dans son propre contexte juridique. Pour ceux qui veulent utiliser le livre comme un manuel de référence, il suffit d'étudier simplement le résumé principal, les titres des chapitres ainsi que les références des publications et les listes de lois et réglementations offerts à la fin du rapport.

Résultats

Ce rapport aborde les sujets juridiques qui se présentent actuellement dans les domaines de la télémédecine et de télématique de santé dans le but d'aider les politiciens, les gestionnaires des systèmes de santé ainsi que les directeurs de projets en télématique de santé. Ce faisant, il lie les questions actuelles de responsabilité juridique, des droits de propriété intellectuelle et de la protection des données sensibles aux directives et actes législatifs européens et aussi aux lois nationales des états membres. Prenant en considération les aspects historiques et culturels sous-jacents, le rapport s'appuie sur des entretiens approfondis et des séances de travail réalisées avec des experts venant des ministères de la santé, des compagnies d'assurance, des associations professionnelles etc. ainsi que sur une analyse universitaire. Les principaux résultats de ce livre proviennent d'un rapport du groupe de travail sur les aspects légaux du projet SIREN («Security in Regional Networks», sécurité dans les réseaux régionaux), qui fut confié à l'ordre des médecins de la Basse-Saxe.

Le rapport fut écrit et édité par un groupe d'experts allemands et belges qui ont travaillé dans le domaine depuis plusieurs années. Ce groupe interdisciplinaire réunit des experts en sécurité technique, des juristes et des experts du droit de la protection des données dans la médecine qui provenaient de trois environnements professionnels différents : Ordre des médecins, cabinets de consultants juridiques internationaux et Université

Il fut ainsi possible de prendre en compte les résultats récents en provenance d'autres études ne participant pas à SIREN, mais qui traitaient du même sujet telles que les études «Enabling Mechanisms» du G7/8 et «Health Data Cards» ainsi que d'une étude aprofondie menée pour la Direction Générale V de la Commission Européenne sur la question des signatures électroniques en Europe, des projets européens,

SEISMED/ISHTAR et TRUSTHEALTH 1, et enfin de l'expérience quotidienne dans plusieurs cabinets de consultants internationaux.

L'étude constate que les problèmes de responsabilité juridique sont un obstacle majeur pour le développement de l'utilisation de la télématique de santé et de la télémédecine. La question de responsabilité juridique est analysée à l'aide de deux exemples assez simples mais particulièrement appropriés:

- la téléconsultation internationale pour un cas de patient donné et
- l'échange international de données relatives aux patients en cas d'urgence.

Ces exemples sont présentés en relation avec sept concepts de responsabilité juridique qui ont été définis et discutés dans le cadre d'une approche multidisciplinaire. Il est décrit pour chaque concept en quoi la signature digitale et le cryptage peuvent améliorer la situation juridique.

Il est apparu que dans la plupart des situations, l'utilisation de signatures électroniques, de tiers de confiance (Trusted Third Party (TTP) et de cryptographie améliore considérablement la situation juridique de la télématique de santé. Cependant, en examinant l'état présent de ces développements dans les différents pays européens et au niveau de l' Europe pour le domaine de la santé, on constate que les concepts de signatures électroniques, de tiers de confiance et de cryptographie n'y sont arrivés que récemment. Sans les structures de sécurité mentionnées ci-dessus, la télématique et la télémédecine ne progresseront pas notablement dans l'avenir. Des actions immédiates et stratégiques sont donc indispensables.

Deux séances de travail juridiques qui eurent lieu vers la fin de l'année 1996 et à l'automne de 1998 révélaient que ni universitaires, ni politiciens ne se rendaient compte de l'importance du développement et de la mise en œuvre de solutions juridiques pour la pratique quotidienne de la télématique. Dans beaucoup de ministères nationaux de la santé, on pensait qu'il s'agissait d'un sujet plutôt général et du ressort des ministères de la justice ou de l'intérieur. Ce rapport, par contre, souligne le fait que dans la plupart des états membres de l'Europe, les traditions culturelles ont favorisé un développement d'une grande variété de législations dans le secteur de la télématique de santé. Par conséquent, il ne parait pas très réaliste de s'attendre à des solutions générales pour les questions précises de responsabilité juridique dans la télématique de santé.

C'est pour cette raison que le rapport recommande aux directeurs de projets de bien considérer le problème dans leurs propositions et leurs projets, car les aspects légaux pourraient bien devenir un obstacle majeur à l'acceptation générale des systèmes télématiques. Le rapport recommande aux politiciens du secteur de la santé de s'intéresser au problème et d'analyser comment les réglementations nationales devraient être adaptées pour permettre l'emploi de signatures électroniques, de techniques de cryptage et de tiers de confiance dans les domaines de la télématique de santé et de la télémédecine. Enfin, le rapport recommande aux experts juristes de préparer des modèles de contrats pouvant être utilisés par les acteurs offrant des services de téléconsultation ou envoyant des données aux médecins traitant s'appuyant sur un *Code de bonne Pratique*. Dans les années à venir, une telle approche systématique pourrait devenir l'élément clé du développement de systèmes de télématique de santé en attendant qu'une réglementation juridique générale plus claire et plus précise soit préparée au niveau de l'Europe et des états membres.

En conclusion, le rapport analyse comment la télématique de santé se transforme de manière dynamique en s'adaptant et en créant des constructions légales pour réglementer la télématique de santé dans la société. Cette approche formelle fait apparaître clairement que quelques lois ou règlements ne pourront guère éclaircir le sujet. Plutôt, l'adaptation juridique doit avoir pour but de s'adapter au développement technique continuel. Le fait que les cycles de développements sont nettement plus longs dans le domaine légal que dans le domaine technique crée des lacunes sujettes à controverse et des terrains d'incertitude.

Recommandations générales concernant le travail futur dans la EC

La prise en compte des aspects les plus importants de ce rapport permet de tirer quelques recommandations générales pour le travail futur concernant les aspects légaux de la télématique de santé pour la Commission Européenne, à savoir des recommandations extraites de celles qui furent formulées d'une manière plus détaillée dans le deuxième session de travail juridique (documentée dans les pages 145/6/7):

1. Du fait de la complexité du sujet, beaucoup de temps sera nécessaire pour harmoniser les réglementations nationales et les accords internationaux des professionnels. Des solutions contractuelles peuvent constituer les premières étapes. Dans le même temps, le développement de Codes de bonne conduite et d'éthique au niveau européen ou au niveau global, est essentiel et urgent pour soutenir le développement de systèmes télématiques nationaux et transfrontaliers.
2. Il y a un besoin urgent de préparer un ensemble de contrats types qui puissent être utilisés entre les patients et les fournisseurs de services dans le domaine de la téléconsultation. Ces contrats type doivent couvrir les situations les plus fréquentes que l'on peut imaginer dans les trois années à venir.
3. Une intense coopération entre les associations des professionnels de santé dans la Communauté européenne est d'un vif intérêt pour commencer une harmonisation des réglementations professionnelles et notamment des procédures d'authentification dans les différents états membres. De plus, il serait extrêmement utile d'harmoniser les procédures d'enregistrement professionnels comme point de départ pour une mise en place progressive des tiers de confiance.

4. Il y a un besoin urgent d'entreprendre une recherche sur les nouveaux aspects légaux soulevés par les développements futurs dans la médecine et la télématique de santé, particulièrement en ce qui concerne les domaines de la médecine moléculaire, le code génétique et les systèmes de réalité virtuelle.
5. La complexité du sujet est aussi impressionnante que la rareté des experts confirmés dans le domaine en question, experts qui soient capables d'intégrer des connaissances profondes en télématique, en droit et en médecine. Ceci explique que les solutions faciles proposées par des projets orientés uniquement sur une approche disciplinaire ne pourront avoir d'impact important. Il importe aussi que les programmes d'enseignement tiennent compte de ce problème.
6. Étant donné le grand intérêt que beaucoup de pays d'outre-mer ont pour une télécoopération avec des institutions européennes dans le secteur de la santé et que la téléconsultation internationale pourrait bien devenir réalité au niveau mondial d'ici quelques années, tous les projets européens devraient prendre en compte le problème légal en poursuivant les développements des projets dits G 7 / G 8 et devraient intégrer des modules de formation des utilisateurs finals dans leurs programmes.
7. En plus de tout action protectrice et de toutes infrastructures comme la signature électronique ou le cryptage, les systèmes légaux ont besoin de prendre des mesures contre la criminalité dans les réseaux, de se prémunir contre la programmation, la distribution et l'exécution de logiciels destructifs, ainsi que contre la violation de la sphère privée.

Resumen

Cuadro

El objetivo del presente informe es analizar de que manera los aspectos legislativos y jurídicos actualmente impactan en el desarrollo de la Telemática en el campo de la salud. Se fundamenta en un intenso diálogo tanto con expertos de disciplinas jurídicas y telemáticas así como tomadores de decisiones en temas relativos a la Salud Pública y directores de proyecto en el campo de la Telemática Médica.

A escala global se podría demostrar por medio de los proyectos llamados G-7/8, cuan eficazmente la Telemática Médica puede apoyar las funciones de la Salud Pública y la Atención Médica. Desde los años 70 se ha discutido el tema de la seguridad informática como uno de los posibles obstáculos al uso extendido de la Tecnología Informática en la Atención Médica. Tanto los projectos europeos del IV° y V° Programa Marco como las experiencias internacionales sugieren que el tema de la seguridad ha alcanzado máxima importancia en la discusión actual sobre telemedicina y redes globales de ordenadores en la sanidad pública. Probablemente cuestiones de derechos de la propiedad intelectual se convertirán en el problema fundamental.

El informe fue escrito como ayuda práctica para el personal de dirección en la Salud Pública y en la Telemática Sanitaria. Proveerá al lector una referencia fácil y rápida sobre los aspectos legales en el contexto de projectos actuales o futuros. Para poder mantener el informe resumido y focalizado solo fueron examinados los ejemplos de la tecnología informática más importantes usados en Telemática Médica.

El informe se estructura en ocho capitulos: Capítulo 1° describe el marco y la hipótesis base del informe presente y analiza la legislación actual. El capítulo 2° presenta la metodología para determinar un modelo de referencia mientras que el capítulo 3° describe los resultados de un estudio sobre el terreno de la responsabilidad referiendose a dos escenarios telemáticos especialmente con miras a cuestiones de responsabilidad. Además ese capítulo da una idea de la situación jurídica de los diferentes paises europeos. El capítulo 4° describe principalmente de que manera los desarollos técnicos en el ámbito de la telemática sanitaria serán incluidos en la legislación y como desde un entendimiento del proceso a largo plazo, pueden derivar las acciones que ayuden a desarrollar soluciones tempranas para problemas legales difíciles. El capítulo 5° se ocupa de temas específicos de la Telemática en Salud como ser el procesamiento de imágenes, la investigación médica o el registro de casos. El capítulo 6° formula recomiendaciones para trabajos futuros. El capítulo 7° es un resumen de las recomendaciones de la Comisión Europea. El capítulo 8° contiene la documentación de varios seminarios sobre ese tema así como un índice de personas y de topicos, que facilita al lector a encontrar rápidamente los pasajes relevantes en el reporte.

El lector que cuente con poco tiempo y que está principalmente interesado en el análisis de la problemática de la telemedicina mientras se siente familiar con las cuestiones jurídicas, directamente podría comenzar con el capítulo 3°. A los colegas que buscan una introducción que los acerque al complejo temático, se les aconseja seguir la secuencia actual del informe. Los profesionales de la salud con mas experiencia que buscan una sistematización de los conocimientos, seguramente interpretarán el contenido del capítulo 4° a su situación jurídica particular. Si desea utilizar el libro como obra de consulta se recomienda la lectura del resumen, de los encabezamientos, de los índices y de las referencias legislativas.

Resultados

El informe aquí presentado trata sobre temas jurídicos actuales del campo de la telemedicina y de la telemática en salud pública, que ayudan a políticos, administradores de salud y lideres de proyectos en Telemática Médica. Combina las cuestiones urgentes de la responsabilidad, del derecho de la propiedad intelectual y de la seguridad informática sobre acciones legislativas y directivas europeas tanto como proyectos legislativos de los paises miembro de la UE. Por un lado el informe basa en extensas entrevistas y seminarios con expertos de la Salud, de seguros, asociaciones profesionales, etc. y por otro lado se funda en análisis investigativos. También refleja sobre aspectos históricos y culturales. El resultado principal de este libro tiene sus orígenes en los "Aspectos legales" de la medida complementaria SIREN ("Security in Regional Networks" - "seguridad en redes regionales"). Este parte del proyecto fue adjudicado al colegio de médicos en Baja Sajonia, Alemania (Niedersächsische Ärztekammer, Deutschland).

El informe fue editado y escrito de un grupo de expertos belga-germano, cuyos miembros trabajan en ese ámbito desde hace años. El grupo interdisciplinario estuvo formado por expertos en seguridad técnica, derecho y seguridad legal en informática médica . Los miembros pertenecían a tres grupos diferentes de profesionales: el colegio de médicos, la consultoría de derecho internacional y el ámbito científico.

Fue también posible incluir otros resultados recientes que no formaban parte de SIREN pero que estaban directamente relacionados con la temática. Hay que mencionar especialmente las experiencias recogidas con los estudios del grupo G-7/8 "Enabling Mechanisms" y "Health Data Cards" y con un estudio extenso de la Comisión Europea (DG XV) que trataba el tema de la firma digital en Europa. Además, los resultados de los proyectos de la UE SEISMED/ISHTAR y TRUSTHEALTH 1 están considerados tanto como experiencias jurídicas de la vida cotidiana de diferentes asesorías internacionales.

El estudio plantea el tema de la seguridad como uno de los principales obstáculos para incrementar el uso de la Telemática y la Telemedicina. El tema de la responsabilidad se explica usando dos ejemplos simples y de actualidad:

- Teleconsulta internacional referiendose a un caso específico
- Intercambio internacional de datos de pacientes en casos de urgencia

Los ejemplos son ilustrados con relación a siete conceptos de responsabilidad dentro del marco de un enunciado interdisciplinario que une a los temas informáticos en la salud pública y el campo del derecho. Para cada concepto se describe si la firma digital y la encriptación pueden mejorar la situación legal.

En la mayoría de los casos, la disponibilidad de firmas digitales y la criptografía, mejoran considerablemente la situación legal en el ámbito de la telemática sanitaria en cuanto existe una infraestructura de seguridad con esquemas confiables. Sin embargo cuando el estudio tenía en cuenta la situación de los desarollos legales en los paises distintos de la UE tanto como la situación jurídica de Europa en ese tema, se mostraba que los conceptos para firma digital tanto como TTP y cryptografía aún estan a los comienzos. No se puede esperar que la telemática y la telemedicina se desarollen ampliamente sin las estructuras de seguridad adecuadas. Se requiere de una acción estratégica inmediata en este sentido.

Dos seminarios tenidos a fines de 1996 y en otoño de 1998 mostraban que ni en el ámbito científico jurídico ni políticos de la Salud tenían en cuenta cuan importante sería el desarollo y la implementación de soluciones legales en la práctica cotidiana de la salud pública. En numerosos Ministerios Nacionales de Salud, clasifican el tema como de interés público y general del que deberían ocuparse los Ministerios de Justicia o los Ministerios del Interior. Así mismo, el informe enfatiza el hecho de que las tradiciones culturales de los paises de la UE conducían a la formación de una multitud de régimenes jurídicos para la salud pública. Por lo tanto, lamentablemente , se podría esperar tan sólo soluciones teóricas generales para los temas sobre la responsabilidad en el campo de la Telemática Médica.

El informe recomienda a los directores de proyectos, que consideren seriamente el tema de la seguridad en sus proyectos y propuestas ya que los aspectos legales pueden convertirse en los principales obstáculos para la aprobación de sistemas telemáticos para la atención médica. Recomienda también a los políticos de la Salud que traten este tema y analicen como podría adaptarse el régimen jurídico nacional para permitir los programas para el uso de firma digital, de la tecnología cryptográfica y de TTP en el ámbito de la telemática, la salud pública y la telemedicina. Por último, recomienda a los expertos en Derecho que formulen contratos modelo para ser utilizados entre las partes preparadas para ofrecer servicios de teleconsulta o enviar información a los profesionales tratantes, basados en Códigos de Buena Práctica. Este acercamiento sistematizado puede ser un elemento fundamental en el desarrollo de sistemas de Telemática Médica en los próximos años, antes de que una clara y estricta reglamentación legal sea formulada y adoptada en Europa y en sus estados miembro.

En conclusión, ese informe presenta un análisis sobre como el desarollo de la telemática dinamicamente se refleja en la adopción y la creación de estructuras legales que regulen la Telemática Médica en la sociedad. Está claro desde lo formal, que unas pocas leyes o regulaciones no clarificarán fundamentalmente este tema. En cambio, la adaptación legislativa deben orientarse a continuar con el desarrollo técnico.

Aquí aparece un problema ya que los ciclos legislativos son considerablemente mas largos que los tecnológicos lo que determina brechas controvertidas y zonas de incertidumbre.

Recomendaciones generales para próximos trabajos en la UE

La descripción de los aspectos más importantes del informe aquí presentado, permite derivar algunas recomiendaciones generales para próximos trabajos considerando aspectos jurídicos de la Telemática Médica para la Comisión Europea. Las recomiendaciones siguientes fueron extraidas del reporte detallado del 2º seminario jurídico tal como se documenta en las páginas 145/6/7:

1. En vista de la complejidad del tema, se necesitará cierto tiempo para armonizar las regulaciones jurídicas nacionales, las convenciones internacionales y las legislaciones privadas.
   Simultaneamente será necesario desarrollar «códigos de buena práctica y de ética» a nivel europeo o global que faciliten el desarollo de sistemas de salud Pública nacionales y así como sistemas que sobrepasen las fronteras.
2. Urge el desarrollo de « contratos modelo » que puedan ser usados para regular la relación entre patientes y "service providers" o diferentes services providers entre si en temas de teleconsultas. Deberían estar adaptados para las soluciones más comunes que puedan presentarse en Telemedicina en los dos o tres próximos años.
3. Una estrecha colaboración entre sociedades profesionales de la Salud es indispensable en la UE para comenzar a armonizar las regulaciones profesionales y la especificación de los procedimientos de autentificación entre los diferentes paises de la UE. Además, una reglamentación de los procedimientos de inscripción profesional sería extremadamente útil constituyendo una base de operaciones sin obstáculos para la realización de servicos TTP.
4. Se requiere la investigación y propuesta de nuevos campos jurídicos para los futuros desarollos de la medicina y de la tecnología telemática, específicamente en relación a la medicina molecular, la decodificación del genoma humano y el desarollo de los sistemas de Realidad Virtual.

5. La complejidad de la materia es enorme así como la escasez de expertos dsiponibles que sean capaces de integrar los conocimientos sobre temas de telemática médica, legislación y medicina. Es necesario adaptar las currículas para considerar estos temas en el futuro.
6. Todos los proyectos europeos deberían ser tratados de manera global, siguiendo así desarollos anteriores de los llamados proyectos G7/8. Deberían tambi;en contener los módulos correspondientes de entrenamiento para usuarios finales. Esto es necesario, porque muchos países fuera de Europa, están interesados en realizar proyectos de tele-colaboración en atención médica con instituciones europeas. La teleconsulta internacional probablemente será una realidad en un futuro cercano.
7. Además de todos los sistemas de protección e infraestructura como las firmas digitales y los métodos de encriptación, los sistemas jurídicos necesitan establecer regulaciones jurídicas contra acciones criminales en redes electrónicas, tales como la distribución y la ejecución de programas destructores así como la violación de la esfera privada.

Sammanfattning

Ramverk

Målet med denna rapport är att belysa hur legala frågor påverkar utvecklingen av medicinsk informatik. Resultatet baseras på en omfattande dialog mellan ett flertal experter på legala frågor och medicinsk informatik. Även policyskapare inom området och projektledare i informatikprojekt har medverkat.

På det globala planet har de så kallade G7/G8 projekten visat hur effektivt medicinsk informatik kan ge stöd i folkhälsosammanhang och i hälso- och sjukvården. Sedan 70-talet har dataskyddsfrågor ibland uppfattats som hinder för en omfattande användning av informationsteknik (IT) i hälso- och sjukvården. I de europeiska projekten inom hälso- och sjukvårdsområdet i fjärde och femte ramprogrammen liksom i den pågående debatten om telemedicin och globala nätverk är de internationella erfarenheterna att ansvarsfrågorna blivit de mest angelägna.

Denna rapport är skriven för att utgöra ett verktyg för dem som arbetar med ledningen av hälso- och sjukvård och medicinsk informatik. Den ger en snabb och enkel referens till relevanta legala frågor i sina sammanhang. För att göra denna rapport kort och koncentrerad så har bara de viktigaste IT exemplen avseende medicinsk informatik belysts.

Rapporten är indelad i åtta avsnitt: Avsnitt 1 beskriver principiella antaganden och gjorda avgränsningar. Detta avsnitt innehåller också en analys av rådande legala förhållanden. Avsnitt 2 beskriver den metodik som använts för att analysera ansvarsförhållanden rörande telemedicin och hur en referensmodell avseende legala aspekter kan skisseras. Avsnitt 3 beskriver relevanta ansvarsförhållanden i två telemedicinska scenarier. De legala förhållandena i olika medlemsstater har studerats. Avsnitt 4 beskriver hur teknisk utveckling inom området medicinsk informatik tas om hand i nya lagar och bestämmelser, men också hur man tidigt kan utveckla lösningar i ny lagstiftning om man förstår den underliggande långsiktiga utvecklingen. Avsnitt 5 tar upp särskilda frågor avseende medicinsk informatik som bilder, medicinsk forskning, hälso- och vårdregister. Avsnitt 6 sammanfattar rekommendationerna för framtida arbete. Avsnitt 7 utvecklar en syn på arbetet i Europa. Avsnitt 8 innehåller dokument från flera arbetsmöten om legala frågor. I avsnittet redovisas relevanta dokument m.m. För att enkelt kunna finna relevanta delar i rapporten finns en lista på namn och ämnen som stöd för läsaren.

Läsare som önskar fokusera på telemedicinområdet kan genast läsa avsnitt 3 om vederbörande har en grundläggande kunskap om områdets legala aspekter. Den som önskar komma in i frågeställningarna efter hand kan läsa rapporten avsnitt för avsnitt. För professionella seniorer som önskar finna en struktur kan säkert tolka innehållet i avsnitt 4 så att det kan utgöra ett stöd för vederbörande. Om läsaren bara vill använda boken som referenslitteratur är det tillräckligt att ta del av denna sammanfattning, innehållsförteckningen och redovisade förteckningar över litteratur, lagar, föreskrifter och råd.

Resultat

Denna rapport beskriver rådande legala förhållanden avseende telemedicin och medicinsk informatik. Den avses ge stöd till politiker, tjänstemän och projektledare inom hälso- och sjukvården. Den kopplar ansvarsfrågor, immaterialrättsliga frågor och dataskydd till europeiska lagliga åtgärder och direktiv men också till nationell lagstiftning i medlemsstaterna. Rapporten som tar hänsyn till underliggande historiska och kulturella aspekter baseras på omfattande intervjuer och diskussioner vid vilka experter från socialdepartement, försäkringsbolag, professionella organisationer etc. deltagit. De viktigaste resultaten i denna bok härrör från "the Legal Workshop in the European Accompanying Measure SIREN (Security in Regional Networks)". Denna del av Sirenprojektet har genomförts av Läkaresällskapet i Niedersachsen i Tyskland.

Rapporten skrevs och redigerades av en grupp tyska och belgiska experter, som har arbetat inom det aktuella området i flera år. Den tvärvetenskapliga gruppen innehöll experter på säkerhetsinformatik, experter på legala frågor och experter på skydd av medicinska data. Personerna kom från olika läkaresällskap, universitet och konsultföretag specialiserade på rättsinformatik i hälso- och sjukvården.

Det har också varit möjligt att relativt sent ta till vara material från olika studier som inte ingick i SIREN, men som berör samma område. Detta har också studerats i G7/G8 projekt som "Enabling Mechanisms" och "Health Data Cards". Motsvarande problemställningar har också studerats i DG XV om digitala signaturer i Europa. EU projekten SEISMED/ISHTAR och TrustHealth 1 liksom i det dagliga arbetet med legala frågor i t.ex. internationella konsultföretag, som arbetar med rättsinformatik inom hälso- och sjukvården behandlar också samma frågeställningar.

Studien har kommit till slutsatsen att ansvarsförhållandena är ett allvarligt hinder för att utöka användningen av medicinsk informatik och telemedicin. Ansvarsförhållandena har analyserats utgående från två ganska enkla men ständigt relevanta exempel:

- internationella telekonsultationer avseende ett givet fall och
- internationellt utbyte av patientdata vid medicinska nödsituationer

Dessa exempel beskrivs i relation till sju ansvarskoncept, som har formulerats och diskuterats i en interdiciplinär ansats. I varje koncept beskrivs om digitala signaturer och kryptering kan förbättra den legala situationen.

Det klarläggs att i de flesta fall så sker en avsevärd förbättring av den legala situationen för medicinsk informatik om tillgängligheten till digitala signaturer och tillförlitliga tredjepartstjänster liksom kryptering kan erhållas. Dessa tjänster har inte förrän helt nyligen kunnat erbjudas. Fortsatt utveckling i medicinsk informatik och telemedicin kan inte utvecklas på bredden utan säkerhetsstrukturer. Det är därför viktigt att snarast vidta nödvändiga strategiska åtgärder.

Två arbetsmöten om legala frågor ett sent 1996 och ett hösten 1998 visade att varken rättsinformatiker inom akademierna eller policyskapare inom hälso- och sjukvården var tillräckligt varse om hur nödvändigt det är att utveckla och implementera legala lösningar i medicinsk informatik i praktiken. I många medlemsstaters socialdepartement ansågs frågorna vara av allmän natur varför de borde tas om hand av respektive justitiedepartement. Denna rapport betonar emellertid det faktum att de kulturella traditionerna i de flesta medlemsstaterna har utvecklats olika beroende på varierande legala regelverk för medicinsk informatik. Det är således bara teoretiskt möjligt att förvänta relevanta gemensamma lösningar avseende typiska ansvarssituationer som finns inom inom hälso- och sjukvården.

Denna rapport rekommenderar projektledare att allvarligt överväga frågorna i sina förslag och projekt då legala aspekter kan bli ett väsentligt hinder för allmän acceptans av medicinsk informatik. Det rekommenderas till policyskapare att ta upp frågor och analysera hur nationella bestämmelser måste anpassas för att tillåta digitala signaturer, tillförlitliga tredjepartstjänster och kryptering inom området medicinsk informatik och telemedicin. Rättsinformatiker rekommenderas utforma modellkontrakt mellan parter som erbjuder konsultation med utnyttjande av telemedicin eller dataöverföring mellan vårdgivarna. Sådana modellkontrakt bör referera till professionens etiska principer och accepterad ”code of conduct”. En sådan systematisk ansats kan bli ett centralt element utvecklingen av system för medicinsk informatik under de kommande åren innan klara och precisa allmänna legala principer har utformats och antagits i EU och i medlemsstaterna.

Slutligen analyseras i denna rapport hur utvecklingen av medicinsk informatik speglas i nya konsultationer där medicinsk informatik används. Av det som sagts är det uppenbart ett litet antal lagar eller regler inte helt kan klarlägga frågan. I stället måste lagstiftningen efter hand i anpassas och vara i paritet med den tekniska utvecklingen . Det faktum att den legala utvecklingen är avsevärt långsammare än den inom IT-området kan bidra till att legala gap och osäkerheter uppkommer.

Allmänna rekommendationer för det framtida arbetet i EU

De viktigaste aspekterna i denna rapport medger att ett antal allmänna rekommendationer för framtida arbete om legala aspekter avseende medicinsk informatik kan tas fram. Dessa kan härledas från de mer detaljerade rekommendationerna från det andra arbetsmötet om legala frågor. De har dokumenterats på sidorna 145/6/7 i denna rapport.

1. Mot bakgrund av frågornas komplexitet behövs avsevärd tid för att harmonisera nationella legala bestämmelser, internationella professionella överenskommelser och privata legala överenskommelser. Under tiden är det nödvändigt att ta fram europeiska eller globala ”codes of good practice” baserade på etiska överväganden. Detta blir sedan ett stöd för utvecklingen av nationella och särskilt transnationella system för medicinsk informatik.
2. En uppsättning modellkontrakt kan upprättas. Dessa kan sedan användas mellan patienter och vårdgivare inom t ex telemedicinområdet där det omedelbart föreligger ett behov. Kontrakten bör täcka de mest vanliga situationerna som kan förväntas inom en två- till treårsperiod.
3. Ett nära samarbete mellan professionella grupper i Unionen är av vitalt intresse för att i medlemsstaterna påbörja harmonisering av regler och särskilt även procedurer för autenticiering av vårdgivare. Dessutom bör en harmonisering av registreringen av professionella grupper inom hälso- och sjukvården bör kunna utgöra en grund till en katalogtjänst, som är en nödvändig del inom de tillförlitliga tredjepartstjänsterna.
4. Forskning om de nya legala frågorna som kommer upp i samband med framtida utveckling inom medicinen och inom området medicinsk informatik särskilt i relation till molekylär medicin, genetik och system för "virtual reality" är central.
5. Frågornas komplexitet är stor liksom bristen på seniorer, som har vilja, kunnande och förmåga att integrera kunskaper om medicinsk informatik, rättsinformatik och medicin. Detta betyder att enkla lösningar som läggs fram av många tekniskt projekt inte kommer att få allmänt stöd. Att anta läroplaner och utbilda inom dessa områden är därför nödvändigt och brådskande.
6. Då många länder i andra världsdelar är intresserade av telemedicinsamarbete med europeiska institutioner kan telekonsulting på global nivå bli realitet om ett fåtal år. Alla europeiska projekt borde ta upp dessa frågor i ett globalt perspektiv och noga följa utvecklingen i G7/G8 projekten som borde innehålla motsvarande utbildningsmoduler.
7. Utöver skyddsåtgärder och infrastruktur som digitala signaturer och kryptering måste lagstiftarna ta upp och diskutera mått och steg för att motverka kriminella aktiviteter i nätverk som program, distribution och exekvereing av destruktiva program liksom åtgärder som bryter patientintegriteten.

The Editors, Key Authors, and Experts

This report was written and in some parts edited by five people together with other European experts. The study was carried out within the EU project SIREN (Security in Regional Networks). In addition, this report contains and reflects many other results of actual studies, too.

Editors and Key Authors:

Otto Rienhoff, Physician, Professor of Medical Informatics, Göttingen, Germany. Rienhoff has been active in the field of data protection since the 1970s and has addressed legal issues in Health Telematics in relation to imaging systems, research, molecular biology, and networked information systems. In the early 1990s he formulated the idea of a patient pointer card as a means to provide control for data subjects over their personal data. Within the SIREN project he led the legal workpackage for the Physicians ChamberPhysicians Chamber of Lower Saxony.

Caroline Laske, Lawyer, International Legal Consultant, Brussels, Belgium. Laske specialised in information technology law and focuses in her research on aspects of comparative law and European Union law. Since the early 1990s she has been involved in a number of European Commission sponsored projects, such as EURIPACS, SEISMED, and ISHTAR, in the context of which she has worked on the development of practical solutions for everyday legal problems in the field of health information systems.

Patrick van Eecke, Lawyer, Interdisciplinary Center for Law and Information Technology, Leuven, Belgium. Van Eecke has been involved in international legal consultancy for several years and in several EU projects. He has greatly contributed to adapting Belgian law to digital signature schemes, and is the editor and key author of the most renowned DG XV report on digital signatures in Europe which became the basis for the European Directive.

Paul Wenzlaff, Mathematician and Scientific Researcher, Center for Quality Management of the Physicians ChamberPhysicians Chamber of Lower Saxony, Hannover, Germany. Wenzlaff was one of the key statistical experts for clinical studies of the Hannover Medical School in Germany in the eighties. In his current position at the Physicians ChamberPhysicians Chamber, he acts as the Chamber's representative in various European national and international securityprojects.

Ursula Piccolo, Psychologist, Research Manager at the Medical Informatics Department, University of Göttingen, Germany. Piccolo has been working in the field of Medical Informatics for about three decades. She has co-edited various books and articles on educational, social and legal aspects of Health Telematics. She is responsible for project activities, project linking, and international exchange.

The Experts:

The editors and key authors would like to thank the participants of the first and second Legal Workshop of SIREN as well as all those experts who contributed to the project by providing written or oral information on legal developments in their country.

First Legal Workshop:

Paper and report prepared by
Marion Herbst (Hannover, Germany); Sandra Schulz (Berlin, Germany).
Participants Rosa Julia-Barceló (Belgium), Tim Benson (United Kingdom); Filip De Meyer (Belgium); Per Furberg (Sweden); Zoi Kardasiadou (Greece); Wolfgang Kilian (Germany); Gunnar Klein (Sweden); Yves Poullet (Belgium).

Second Legal Workshop:

Paper and report prepared by
Ben A. Stanberry (Cardiff, United Kingdom)
Participants François-André Allaert (France); Ab Bakker (The Netherlands); Jan Jaap Bos (The Netherlands); Alistair Donaldson (United Kingdom); Christina Friede-Mohr (Germany); Per Furberg (Sweden); Zoi Kardasiadou (Greece); Henrik Marstrand (Denmark); Jacques Nouwt (The Netherlands); Jacques Sauret (France); Scott Sinclair (United Kingdom); Peter van Osch (The Netherlands); Albert van der Werff (Belgium); Petra Wilson (United Kingdom).

Other Experts:

Tim Benson (United Kingdom); Alfred Büllesbach (Germany); Giovanni Buonomo (Italy); Sigrun Erber-Faller (Germany); José Torres Huertas (Spain); Joaquim Lupi (Portugal).

Christian Dierks (Germany) made the executive summary of the Einbeck Workshop available for this report.

We give our thanks to Katja Nennstiel, Gabriele Scheel and Janko Verhey from Göttingen as well as Nora Oliveri from Argentina and Toleif Ollhede from Sweden for compiling this text and for the translations into French, Spanish and Swedish.

Parts of this book have been cited and used in other contexts by some of the many contributors. This has led to more and more requests for the complete documentation.

We acknowledge the funding by the European Commission (DG XIII) for the SIREN Legal Workpackage under the EU-Project Officers: Gottfried Dietzel (1996); Petra Wilson (1996-1999), and Irmgard Heiber (1999).

1. Digital Signatures and Encryption as Key Elements of Security in Health Telematics

1.1. General Considerations

Addressing Leaders in Health Care

Interdisciplinary reports often face the difficulty of not being accepted in the „clean" environments of conventional schools of thought. This specifically applies to the medical and the legal fields. In view of the interdisciplinary character of the readers, this report makes use of various editorial techniques used in the different sectors. This will allow readers from those sectors to find some familiar structures and elements. However, the prime purpose of the report is to address project leaders, health managers, health professionals, and politicians who wish to update their knowledge on how to facilitate more cost-effective health care services through the use of information technology (IT).

Basic Assumptions Guiding this Report

A report of this type has to reflect some basis assumptions about roles and responsibilities in a complex health care system. These issues are debated differently in each country because of diverse cultural and historical roots. Underlying in this report are the following basic principles regarding patients and health professionals:

Patient orientation

Activities in the health care sector are oriented towards the improvement of the status of patients or engaged in preventive medicine. Patients should control diagnostic, therapeutic, or teaching procedures as well as research to which they may be subject.

Health professional as a patient's partner

The key partner for the patient is the health professional, often the physician on whom the patient depends in all cases of emergency, critical illness, unconsciousness, and weakness of mind or body. The health professional is therefore the cornerstone for the trustworthiness of the health care system for the patient.

Quality equals monetary efficiency

The regulation for the use of IT in health care will, among others, be guided by the notions of cost and quality, with quality being the key factor for the sick individual.

Ethical Issues and Codes of Conduct

Ethical codes have a long tradition in computer science, especially in the Anglo-Saxon common law context. The International Federation of Information Processing (IFIP) was the first international organisation to publish an international code of ethics on how to properly use information technology (IT). This discussion has continued in several member countries of IFIP and is still growing.

The International Medical Informatics Association (IMIA)[1] decided during its 1998 8th Global Conference in Seoul, Korea, to focus on the issue of drawing up a code of ethics in the field of Health Telematics. This work has been allocated to Working Group 4 of IMIA, currently headed by Professor A. Bakker from the The Netherlands. The work shall conclude with the first draft after a working conference in Victoria, Canada, in the year 2000[2].

It is interesting to observe that codes of ethics and codes of professional conduct seem to become the earliest form of regulative norms in international technical or medical developments. However, such codes are still both very recent and little understood regarding their international impact so that further research is considered as appropriate.

Besides the traditional concept of data protection liability concepts, and intellectual property rights there are further legal aspects of the emerging information society in health care, which have as yet not been fully ascertained:

- the legal identity of learning and self-developing software tools (e.g. learning agents acting in the net;
- the legal character of molecular personal information and its relation to legal regulations in the technical informatics world;
- the legal interpretation of activities with modified copies of real individuals in a virtual environment;
- and other.

These are mentioned at the beginning of this report so as to demonstrate that exiting legal questions will accompany the development of Health Telematics in the future.

An important aspect of the discussion has been various forms of the ethical and legal interpretations of the so-called human analogue. This concept, firstly published by Kluge in 1990[3], has been followed up by several authors in regard to coding in relation to medical documentation, medical imaging, virtual reality and publication in health care.

---

[1] http://www.imia.org
[2] Security of the Distributed Electronic Patient Record (EPR) - 8th Working Conference of the International Medical Informatics Association Working Group 4, June 21 - 24, see : http://hinf.uvic.ca/imia_wg4/.
[3] IMIA WG I conference, Victoria, Canada 1990

At the centre of this debate is the question of how to deal with data sets which map a human being in such a way as to create a data model of the individual. Subsequently, this data model relates and impacts on the original. This is particularly relevant when the mapping process is not valid or reliable. Thus conclusions are drawn from the data model, while the impact of the decision will affect the original.

A similar discussion is raised by information models of human beings which describe them to such a degree that it becomes determinable. An example would be molecular biology research, an issue already known from the days of conventional medical archiving, e. g. with respect to Chorea Huntington families.

The ethical and legal discussions in this field do not only relate to conventional data objects as we know them in the computer world, but also to lab specimens or parts of the human body which, with the help of genetic analysis, can deliver important information about an individual. These issues are seen as increasingly relevant and important. Awareness of this was raised, for example, in Germany during three workshops on the issue in 1999.[4]

Definition of terms

In the context of ethics, a number of notions are frequently used with diverse meanings or connotations in different countries or cultures. For example, the term „medicine“ is closely linked to physicians in the Anglo-American world and nearly identical to „health“ in the French or German context. Other examples are the different meanings of terms like „symptom“ or „sign“ in German, English, and French.

In the legal context three terms are regularly used despite different meanings and connotations in different languages as summarised in Tab. 1. Most prominent is the phrase “Deontology” which is in the medical context primarely rooted in the French language.

[4] The most focused one was the workshop “Telematics in Telemedicine - Ethical questions regarding future communication technology” of the famous Loccum Academie, currently in print.

Tab. 1: Different definitions of relevant terms to this report in some languages. Definitions are extracted from Webster's, New York 1989; Petit Larousse Illustre, Paris, 1990; Brockhaus Enzyklopedia, Leipzig, 1977

Term	**Language Culture**	**Definition**
Deontology	English	Ethics, esp. that branch dealing with duty, moral obligation, and right action
	French	Déontologie: Ensemble des règles et des devoirs qui régissent une profession, la conduite de ceux qui l´exercent, les rapports entre ceux- ci et leurs clients ou le public. Déontologie médicale
	German	Special sector of ethical theory (Ethik als Pflichtenlehre) (historical)
	European Projects	Similar to French definition
Ethical Issues	English	1. Pertaining to or dealing with morals or the principlesof morality; 2. pertaining to right and wrong in conduct. 3. In accordance with the rules or standards for right conduct or practice, esp. the standards of a profession...
	French	Foundations of social life, part of philosophy
	German	Principle value issues in societal life, usually defined in very abstract meanings
	European Projects	Confusingly used
Legal Issues	English	1. Permitted by law; lawful 2. Pertaining to law; connected with the law or its administration: the legal profession. 3. Appointed, established, or authorised by law; deriving authority from law....
	French	Lawful
	German	Very much oriented towards codified law
	European Projects	Used in relation to pragmatic juridical issues

1.2. Positioning Health Telematics into the Actual Legal Framework

1.2.1. Are there new Legal Issues in Telemedicine?

Many issues raised by the legal discussions about Health Telematics applications look familiar from a historical viewpoint. They are summarised in the following table. Many are in fact quality issues: in a given historical context the quality of a physician's practice is often ascertained by their governing authorities. It is obvious that some „new" problems have actually existed for decades or centuries in different environments.

Tab. 2: Comparison of organisation, legal aspects and quality management in history and today in relation to health professionals (HP)

Historical Context	Quality Problem	Regulation	Analogy in Health Telematics
Middle Ages	HP moving before liability issues could be raised	None, but rich patients preferred settled physicians, if possible trained monks, Jews or Arabs	Electronic authentication of HP in a networked "anonymous" system through certification authorities and use of digital signatures
USA, Wild West; Germany, 18th century.	HP moving before liability issues could be raised	Certification procedures for locally established and controlled physicians	Save identification of any activity, data-origin etc. in a networked health care environment
Belgium, Germany 1930s	Treatment of patients via telephone	Physicians are not allowed to tele-treat patients	Clear definition of any type of telemedicine activities in contractual form prior to action
Many countries	Dangerous advertise-ment for patients	HPs are not allowed to advertise specific skills	Rules of conduct in networked health services
all times	Untrained individuals offer any service to patients	Certification and registration of HPs	Cross-certified registration schemata in European Member States or international

Thus, for the current legal debates on Health Telematics one may interpret existing and proven rules for the new information technology rather than try to draw up new rules for complex health care issues as some politicians tend to do it[5]. While the first approach allows quick and easy adjustments throughout the development of the information society, the latter, however, offers the potential of European harmonisation for legal regulations in health care. In that sense it could have a similar impact on European health care as the Flexner Report had on American health care at the beginning of this century.

From a legal point of view telemedicine may rapidly reach the status of expert systems in health care: not to use such technology in a critical case may amount to negligence.

Historically, the liability issue has received momentum in the US since the 1960s. Regarding telemedicine the issue of liability is one of the legal issues that increasingly raises attention (see chapter 3.). It is expected that telemedicine will substantially improve service for patients and that the emerging market may raise new liability problems.

The question of whether general security solutions are adequate for the health care sector has always been controversial. On the one hand, protagonists of electronic commerce solutions argue that „solutions save enough for your money are save enough for your health“. On the other hand, arguments are put forward in favour of protecting individual patients in the complex workflows and structures of health care systems through tailored security solutions.

The latter idea is also the basis of many specific and detailed regulations in existing legal systems which safeguard patients rights in conventional paper and pencil environments.

1.2.2. International Legal Approaches to Health Telematics

Several legal instruments have recently been developed internationally to safeguard the emerging information society in general, and in some cases specifically the health care sector. These instruments are propelling national legal action.

In this context the current report also reflects the conclusions of the 1st expert consultation of the World Health Organisation on Telemedicine and its working report: A Health Telematics Policy[6].

---

[5] Ernst Bruckenberger, Ministry of Social Affairs, Lower Saxony, Germany: „The relentless reformists of the health care system, respectively the hospital organization, often resemble people permanently throwing stones of reformation into the sea of objective conditions (demanding attitude, increasingly aging population, progress in medicine, etc.). Seen from the sea, each stone merely rises its level, whereas the persons throwing the stones conclude from the waves on the surface that they have moved something.“ (Zeno; Krankenhausgipfel 1999)

[6] Report of the WHO Group Consultation on Health Telematics 11-16 December, Geneva, 1997 (WHO/DGO/98.1)

1.2.3. European Legal Framework[7]

The European documents can be downloaded from http://Eúropa.EU.int

The following European legal instruments (left column) address the health care sector or have a direct impact on it:

regarding Confidentiality of Communication

95/46/EC	Directive on the protection of individuals with regard to the processing of personal data and the free movement of such data - good data, fair use, privacy, fair access, responsibility
97/66/EC	Directive on the processing of personal data and the protection of privacy in the telecommunication sector - prohibit listening, tapping or storing, erase traffic data, consent to marketing use
R(97)5	Council of Europe Recommendation on the protection of medical data

regarding Electronic Documents

COM(1998)297	Directive on Electronic Signatures (adopted on 13.11.99 by Council) - define essential requirements for electronic signature certificates and certification services, minimum liability rules for services providers - stipulate that an electronic signature could not be legally discriminated against solely on the grounds that it is in electronic form - legal recognition of electronic signatures irrespective of the technology used
COM(1998)585	Green paper on Access to Public Sector Information - improve transparency, access, and fair pricing

regarding Consumer Protection / Liability

92/59/EEC	Directive on the General Product Safety - no-fault liability system on the producer

[7] This list is based on an early version by Petra Wilson, at that time: DG XIII,B1 of Nov. 1998. It was extended during a workshop in Bruxelles in March 1999.

- the onus of proof is on the producer to show that the harm not to arise from the use of his good

93/42/EEC Directive on Medical Devices

- A medical device is any instrument, apparatus, appliance, material or article whether used alone or in combination, including software necessary for its proper application intended to be used on human beings for the purposes of diagnosis, prevention, monitoring, treatment or the alleviation of disease, injury or handicap or control of conception

COM(1998)586 Draft Directive on Electronic Commerce

- liability of intermediaries, exemption for 'mere conduits'
- dispute settlement schemes

regarding Service Provision / Citizen Access

95/62/EC Directive on the application of open network provision to voice telephony

- EU Universal Service Obligation

98/10/EC Directive on the application of open network provision to voice telephony and on universal service for telecommunications in a competitive environment

- Guaranteed provision of service

97/7/EC Directive on the protection of consumers in respect of distance contracts

- right to written information about contracts, right to withdraw

regarding Internet Content

21/12/1998 Action Plan Promoting Safer Use of Internet

- non-regulatory initiatives
- hotlines
- self-regulation
- filtering
- special emphasis on content harmful to children

regarding Cryptography

OECD 1997 — Recommendation of the Council concerning guidelines for cryptography policy and Guidelines for Cryptography Policy, 27 March 1997

- remove, or avoid creating in the name of cryptography policy, unjustified obstacles to international trade and the development of information and communications networks
- promotion of international co-operation between governments

Wassenaar 1996 — Arrangement on Export Controls for Conventional Arms and Dual-Use Goods and Technologies, revised in 1998.

- export restrictions on cryptography signed by 33 countries
- all cryptography products of up to 56 bits key length are free for export,
- mass-market cryptography software and hardware of up to 64 bits key length are free for export,
- the export of products that use encryption to protect intellectual property is relaxed
- export of all other cryptography still requires a license

3381/94 EC — EU Dual-Use of goods regulation (amended by Regulation (EC) 837/95 of April 1995) and EU Council Decision No. 94/942/CFSP (last amended by Council Decision 98/232/CFSP)

- license is needed for the export of cryptography hardware and software outside of the EU. An exception exists for the export of mass-market and public-domain software.
- for a transitional period, the Regulation also requires a licence procedure for intra-Community trade of cryptography products

regarding Computer Criminality

R (89) 9 — Council of Europe Recommendation on computer-related crime of 1990

- stimulates the member states to legislate on computer criminality
- lists the possible computer crimes (hacking, data manipulation, ...)

R (95) 13 Council of Europe Recommendation concerning problems of criminal procedure law connected with information technology of 1995

- stimulates the member states to adapt current procedural law to new technologies
- lists the necessary legal instruments (seizure of data, network search…)

1.2.4. Implementation Process of EU Legal Instruments into National Legislation

To understand the process of how theoretical concepts on legal security in regional networks become implemented into national regulations, it is necessary to know how the European "gearbox" works. From the early stages of initiatives the EU legal instruments follow an implementation process on national ground as can be seen in Figure 1. It is difficult to predict the implementation time scale given the diverse nature of the issue to be regulated, the different national policies and political cultures (see also chapter 4 in this context).

Fig. 1: Procedure of how European legal instruments are developed on European level and implemented on national level in case of regulations for digital signatures and cryptography in correspondence with electronic patient records. The migration path from legal initiatives on the European level to legal regulations on national or regional level is formally easy but complex in reality and results. Experience shows that it is difficult to predict how much time is needed for the migration, depending on issues, countries, and political cultures.

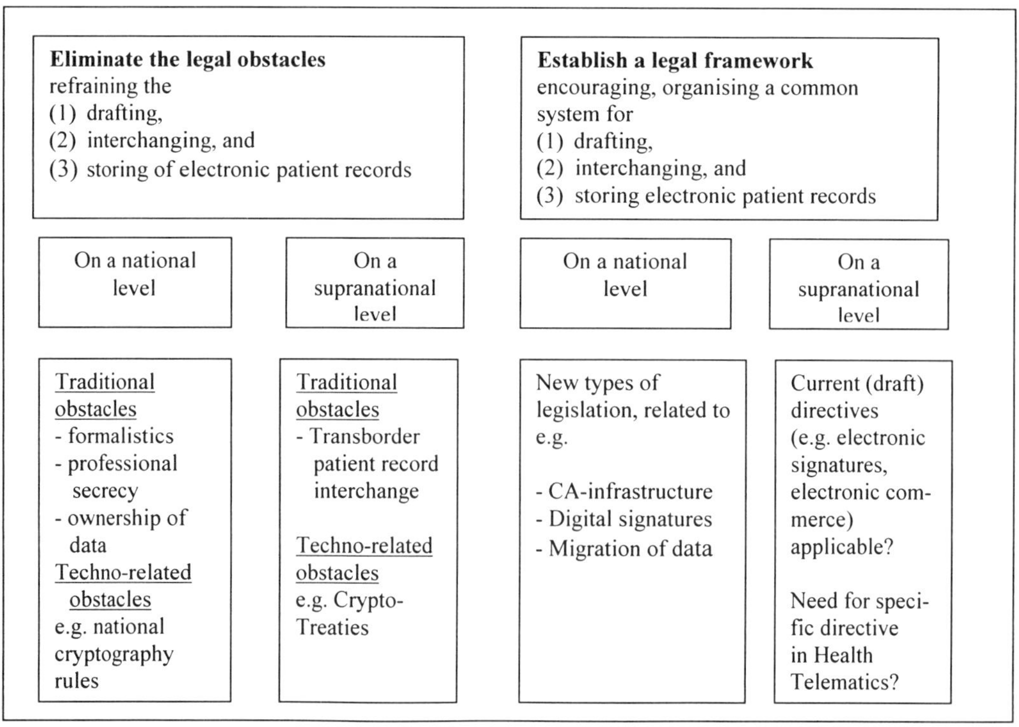

1.2.5. Liability and Evidence - Today's Main Legal Issues in Health Telematics

The increasing implementation and reliance on Health Telematics technology inevitably raises new legal issues. The paper analogy may be helpful and relevant in relation to some new legal questions (e.g. in the context of electronic patient records), but the innovation of technology goes hand in hand with new and/or different types of legal concepts that need to be dealt with away from the paper analogy. In this book, some of the new liability issues are discussed, but it was thought important to place the debate first into a general context of legal developments in relation to the use of telematics technology.

The SIREN study identified four legal concepts as the most relevant in the past and for the future of Health Telematics:

- data protection
- intellectual property rights,
- liability,
- evidence/legal recognition of digital documents and processes.

The debate of both data protection and intellectual property in relation to IT had materialised some decades ago and had undergone a number of national and international legislative processes. Both concepts were defined within a proper framework for most of the known issues. Technological developments have brought about new requirements and raised new issues. Thus, the notions of data protection and intellectual property, although generally established and ascertainable legal concepts, need to be further adapted to the developments (see also chapter 4).

Historically data protection has its roots in the human rights notion of privacy protection. The debate began in the 1960s and gained in momentum in particular in the late eighties and nineties. Today we are in an era post 1995 Data Protection Directive and there is still much uncertainty about its implementation and interpretation. Therefore, the next few years will bring about some changes in the regulation of data protection following national implementations and judicial interpretation in both national courts and the European Court of Justice. Parallel to this process, adjustments will have to be made since it will become evident that the 1995 Directive was not drafted on basis of today's technical realities.

In contrast hereto, issues of liability, evidential cogency and legal recognition of digital documents and processes in relation to Health Telematics have not been as intensively in the arena of legal discussion. This means that both the framework of the debate and of some of the suggested solutions are still insufficiently defined and ascertainable. Hence the debate on these issues is different in nature, more immature and at times still confused.

A first example on the European level is the "97/66 Privacy in the Telecommunication Directive" which needed to fill the telecommunication gap left open by the 1995 Directive. Hence the data protection landscape of the next few years is, despite a substantial body of law, difficult to map out at this stage.

Intellectual property in relation to IT has also solicited a number of legislative initiatives, in particular on international level (beyond the EU). So far, legislation has been drafted based on the paper analogy and hence copyright was thought most appropriate to offer effective protection of software and data bases. New IT products may well require a rethink on this issue. For example, it could be envisaged that robotics products may require patent protection or possibly trademark security.

The debate on liability and evidence/legal recognition of digital documents/processes in relation to Health Telematics has a considerably shorter history in comparison to the two issues mentioned above. The general awareness of and discussion on these questions have intensified over the last few years. We are dealing with extremely vast subjects covering various spheres and a great number of legal principles. This wide-spread diversity and the relative immaturity of the discussions means that, at this point in time, no general framework of discussion and research is as yet clearly identifiable. However, the SIREN study has singled out a number of legal issues that the authors thought essential in relation to the use and implementation of digital signature and encryption technologies in Health Telematics .

1.3. Actual Situation on European Level

This chapter discusses the legal instruments which are either directly relevant to Health Telematics or address several sectors including health care. Each instrument is considered from the following point of views: historical, contents, relevance for Health Telematics, and advantages/ disadvantages.

1.3.1. EU Directive on a Common Framework for Electronic Signatures

History of the Proposal

On 16 June 1998 the European Commission officially submitted a proposal for a European Parliament and Council Directive on a common framework for electronic signatures (COM (1998) 297 final).[8]

---

8 O.J. 23 September 1998, C 325/04-11.

The EU Directive is a response to the in October 1997 adopted communication "Towards A European Framework for Digital Signatures and Encryption."[9] This Communication aims at developing a policy framework with a view to:

- establishing a European framework for digital signatures;
- ensuring the functioning of the Internal Market for cryptographic products and services as well as products and services incorporating cryptographic techniques, while respecting public security concerns and contributing to a homogenous security area in the EU, as set out by the Amsterdam European Council [Presidency Conclusions on freedom, security and justice, Amsterdam European Council, 16/17.6.97];
- stimulating a European industry for cryptographic services and products;
- addressing the international questions raised by the global nature of the Internet and other electronic networks, in particular by removing trade barriers for cryptographic services and products and achieving as far as possible end-to-end communication security on a global scale;
- providing the basis for integration of cryptography within the framework of other European policies such as protection of privacy, consumer interests and intellectual property rights; stimulating and enabling users in all economical sectors to benefit from the opportunities of the global information society which can only be fully exploited if based on a framework of trust and security.[10]This Communication was a followed-up in April 1997 by the Commission Communication "A European Initiative in Electronic Commerce"[11]. This initiative aims at ensuring a common legal framework encompassing the legal recognition of Digital Signatures in the Single Market, the setting up of minimum criteria for Certification Authorities, as well as pursuing world wide agreements. In this Communication the European Commission expresses the need for a sound and flexible regulatory framework which would generate *confidence* for both business and consumers and ensure full and unlimited *access* to the Single Market.

Such a regulatory framework is an essential key to successful European integration as well as a major competitive advantage in itself.[12] The need for a proper legal and technical framework for digital signature technology on European level was further reiterated by the Bonn Ministerial Conference of 6-8 July 1997.[13]

---

9 Communication from the Commission to the European Parliament, the Council, the Economic and Social Committee and the Committee of the Regions ensuring security and trust in electronic communication, Towards A European Framework for Digital Signatures And Encryption", 08/10/97, COM(97)503, (Complete text available at http://www.ispo.cec.be/eif/policy/97503toc.html)

10 COM 97(503), par.10.

11 European Commission, Communication to the European Parliament, the Council, the Economic and Social Committee and the Committee of the Regions, A European Initiative in Electronic Commerce, 15/04/97, COM(97) 157, par. 51; (Complete text available at http://www.cordis.lu/esprit/src/ecomcomx.htm)

12 COM(97) 157, p. 13.

13 http://www2.echo.lu/bonn/conference.html

On 1 December 1997, the Council invited the Commission to submit a proposal for a directive on digital signatures as soon as possible.[14] In April 1998, an expert hearing was organised in Denmark to clarify specific questions on the development and use of digital signatures and encryption and to discuss the text of the EU Directive.[15]

The current proposal aims at ensuring the proper functioning of the internal market in the field of electronic signatures by creating a harmonised and appropriate legal framework for their use. The proposal is based essentially on the following principles[16]:

1. ensuring technological neutrality. Although the proposal concentrates on digital signature technologies employing public-key cryptography, it claims to be technology-neutral and therefore does not focus only on those kinds of signatures
2. avoiding any prior authorisation scheme for the provision of authentication services (intervening in the digital signature) so as not to limit the supply of such services and technological innovation, whilst permitting the introduction of voluntary accreditation schemes for providers of such services with the aim of supplying enhanced levels of security recognising the legal validity of an electronic signature, by preventing it from being denied solely on the grounds that it is in the form of electronic data, and guaranteeing that it is considered equivalent to a hand-written signature if it meets a certain number of conditions.

After elaboration of the texts by the Working Group on Telecommunications of the Council and the Committee of Permanent representatives[17] a final proposal was submitted to the Council of Ministers for political agreement on its meeting held in Brussels on 27 November 1998.[18]

A political agreement could, however, not be reached on the Directive and the Permanent Committee was thus instructed to further elaborate the file. The most important reason for not agreeing on the proposal was the lack of consensus between the Member States on the need for the requirements regarding the quality of the products used to create an electronic signature with full legal effect. On the 22nd of April 1999 the Council of Ministers on its meeting held in Luxembourg agreed on an amended text. A common position of the European Parliament is also soon expected.

---

14 European Commission, Working draft of directive on a Framework for Electronic Certification Services, as published in BNA, Electronic Commerce and Law, March 4, 1998, p.307. See also http://europa.eu.int/comm/dg15/en/index.htm or http://www.law.kuleuven.ac.be/icri for the final draft.
15 http://www.fsk.dk/fsk/div/hearing
16 Report from COREPER (13198/98) on 18 November 1998
17 The European Parliament delivered its opinion on 13 January 1999, the Economic and Social Committee gave its opinion on 2 December 1998, the Committee of the Regions delivered its opinion on 13 January 1999.
18 The proposed directive is based on article 57 (2) concerning the freedom of establishment, article 66 on the freedom to provide services and the approximation rule of article 100 A of the Treaty establishing the European Community. The legislative procedure laid down in article 189b of the Treaty is being followed.

The final version of the directive has been adapted by EU Council of Ministers on the 30th of November 1999.

The Contents of the Directive

The text of the Draft Directive of 16 June 1998 differs in many matters from the final draft which was proposed to the Council of Ministers on 22 April 1999. The most important changes relate to the legal value of an electronic signature. The following description is based on the official final draft as proposed to the Council of Ministers on 22 April 1999.

Article 1: scope

Article 1 describes the scope of the Directive. The Directive aims both at facilitating the use of electronic signatures as well as contributing to their legal recognition. It establishes a legal framework for electronic signatures and certain certification services in order to promote the proper functioning of the internal market. The Directive explicitly states that it does not cover aspects related to the conclusion and validityof contracts or other legal obligations where there are form requirements prescribed by national or Community law. Neither does the Directive affect rules and limits governing the use of documents contained in national or community law.

Article 2: definitions

Article 2 contains a few definitions. Noteworthy is the non-use of the term « digital signature », instead the Directive chooses for a distinction between «electronic signature » and « advanced electronic signature ».

An electronic signature is defined as « data in electronic form attached to, or logically associated with, other electronic data and which serves as a method of authentication ». The term « authentication » itself is neither defined nor explained.

An « advanced electronic signature » is an electronic signature fulfilling a few requirements, which are :

- the signature should be uniquely linked to the signatory;
- the signature is capable of identifying the signatory;
- the signature is created using means that the signatory can maintain under his sole control;
- the signature is linked to the data to which it relates in such a manner that any subsequent alteration of the data is detectable.

Furthermore, the notions « signatory », « signature creation device », « signature verification device », « certificate », « qualified certificate », « certification service provider », and « electronic signature product » are defined.

A signatory is « a person who holds a signature creation device and acts either for himself or the entity he represents ».

A signature creation device is « unique data, such as codes or private cryptographic keys, or a uniquely configured physical device, which is used in verifying the electronic signature. » A signature verification device is *mutatis mutandis* defined in the same manner.[19]

A certificate means « a digital attestation which links a signature verification device to a person, and confirms the identity of that person ». A qualified certificate means « a certificate which meets the requirements laid down in Annex I and is provided by a certification service provider that fulfils the requirements laid down in Annex II.

- The obligations of Annex I laying down the criteria for qualified certificates are requirements relating to the contents of the certificate, such as an indication that the certificate is issued as a qualified certificate,
- the identification of the certification service provider,
- the name of the holder or a pseudonym,
- the possibility to include a specific attribute of the holder depending on the function of the certificate,
- the mention of the beginning and the end of the validity of the certificate,
- the unique identity code of the certificate,
- the advanced electronic signature of the certification service provider issuing the qualified certificate,
- applicable limitations on the scope of the certificate, and
- applicable limitations on the value of transactions for which the certificate can be used.

A certificate answering the mandatory requirements of Annex I will be regarded as a qualified certificate only if it has been issued by a certificate service provider complying with the obligations of Annex II. Annex II states that a certification service provider issuing qualified certificates must :

- demonstrate the necessary reliability for offering certification services,
- ensure the operation of a prompt and secure directory and secure and immediate revocation service,
- verify by appropriate means the identity and if applicable any specific attributes of the person to which a qualified certificate is issued,
- employ competent personnel,
- use trustworthy systems and products,

19 The February 1999 directive text ads the term "secure signature creation device" which is a signature creation device meeting some technical security requirements summed up in an Annex III of the directive. The requirements are focused on the uniqueness, secrecy and protection of the signature creation data and on the assurance that secure devices cannot alter the data to be signed nor prevent that the data can be presented to the signatory before signing.

- take measures against forgery of certificates and protect the confidentiality of secret keys if the service itself generates the secret key
- maintain sufficient financial resources, especially to bear the risk of liability for damages
- record all relevant information concerning a qualified certificate for an appropriate period of time, in particular for evidential purposes;
- not store or copy private signature keys of the customers;
- before entering a contractual relationship inform the customer about the conditions for the use of the certificate, the procedure for complaints, etc.

Article 3: market access principle

Article 3 of the Directive describes the market access principle related to certification services and products for electronic signatures. Member states may not make the provision of certification services subject to prior authorisation. They are, however, allowed to introduce or to maintain voluntary accreditation schemes for the purposes of an enhanced level of certificate services. The conditions related to the accreditation must, however, be objective, transparent, proportionate and non-discriminatory. Furthermore, Member States may not limit the number of accredited certification service providers.

Member states are also obliged to implement a supervisory system to control the certification service providers established on its territory and issuing qualified certificates.

With respect to the use of electronic signatures in the public sector, Member states are allowed to make them subject to additional requirements if these requirements are objective, transparent, proportionate and non-discriminatory, and only relate to the specific characteristics of the application concerned .

Noteworthy is the fact that the Commission may establish and publish reference numbers of generally recognised standards for electronic signature products (article 3, par.3). A product complying with a recognised standard will be presumed to meet the security requirements of the signature creation devices and of the signature products used by the certification service provider.

Article 4: internal market principle

The principles of the Internal Market are addressed in Article 4 of the Directive. Concerning certification services it is stated that a Member state shall only apply national legislation which is in conformity with the Directive to certification service providers established on its territory. Member states may not restrict the provision of certification services that originate in another Members state either.

Article 4 also obliges the Member states to ensure that electronic signature products complying with the directive are permitted to circulate freely within the Internal Market.

Article 5: legal recognition

Article 5 is a core element in the Directive. This article describes the possible legal effects an electronic signature can be appended to in the Internal Market.

Member states have to take care that advanced electronic signatures based on a qualified certificate satisfy the legal requirement of a signature in relation to data in electronic form in the same manner as a hand-written signature satisfies that requirement in relation to paper-based data. These signatures shall also be admissible as evidence in legal proceedings.

Furthermore, the legal effectiveness and the admissibility as evidence in legal proceedings of ordinary electronic signatures may not be denied solely on the grounds that the signature is not in electronic form, or is not based upon a qualified certificate or is not based upon a qualified certificate issued by an accredited certification service provider. The question whether or not the legal effect of an electronic signature should also depend on some minimum product requirements, mentioned in Annex III of the Directive, is an important object of discussion and is the main reason for the failure to reach a political agreement during the Council meeting of 27 November 1998.[20]

Currently, a viable agreement between the Member states is being sought from within the appropriate bodies. It may be expected that a diplomatic solution will resolve the problem by giving Annex III the status of a strong recommendation, or by minimising the product requirements of Annex III.

Article 6: liability

A liability regime for certification service providers is established in Article 6 of the Directive. This liability regime only applies to certification service providers issuing a qualified certificate. It does not matter whether the certification service provider meets the requirements of Annex II or not. Member states are obliged to ensure that a certification service provider is liable for the accuracy of the contents of the qualified certificate, for the assurance of the link between the signature verification device and the signatory, and for the assurance that, when the certification service provider provides the signature devices, the signature creation device and signature verification device are functioning together in a complementary manner.

---

20 The main reason for the non-agreement between some Member States during the Council meeting of 27 November 1998 is that some Member States (Germany, France, Italy) only want to give legal effect to electronic signatures which are created using products that meet a minimum level of technical security. These product security requirements are described in an Annex III, stating that a signature creation device shall reach a minimum level of functional security by appropriate technical and procedural means. Other Member States (especially the United Kingdom and the Netherlands) are opposing obligatory product requirements. The most important reason for this opposition is the fear that by requiring high level security, the industrial market will not be able to meet the conditions. Hence, the directive would risk to refrain the use and development of electronic signatures instead of promoting it.

Important is that the certification service provider can also be held liable for damage to third parties reasonably relying on the certificate, for failure to register revocation of the certificate.

In both cases, certification service providers are not liable when they can prove that they have not acted negligently.

Article 7: international aspects

Article 7 covers the international aspects of the Directive. Certificates issued to the public as qualified certificates by a foreign certification service provider (i.e. established outside the European Union), can be recognised as qualified certificates within the European Union in three cases : a) the issuer in the third country meets the requirements of the Directive and is accredited by a Member state in the context of a voluntary accreditation scheme, b) the foreign certificate is guaranteed by a European Union certification service provider fulfilling the requirements of the Directive, and c) the certificate or the certification service provider is recognised in the context of a bilateral or multilateral agreement between the European Union and third countries or international organisations. Related to the legal recognition of electronic signatures originating in third countries, Article 7 gives the European Commission the task to make proposals for the implementation of standards and international agreements.

Technical translations of the legal requirements

The legal requirements which are defined in the Directive and specifically in its technical annexes (Appendix X 4) are translated into technical terms by the European Electronic Signature Standardization Initiative (EESSI). EESSI is sponsored by the European Commission (DXIII) and Centre Europèen de Normalisation (CEN) and the European Telecommunication Standardization Institute (ETSI). The results of the ESSI are expected to be implemented by vendors of electronic signature products and services (Appendix X4).

Article 8: data protection

Data protection rules are incorporated in Article 8 of the Directive. Interesting is that certification service providers issuing certificates to the public, may collect personal data only directly from or with the explicit consent of the data subject. Further important is that Member states may not prevent certification service providers to indicate a pseudonym in the certificate instead of the signatory 's name.

The other articles deal with the formation of an advisory "Electronic Signature Committee" composed of the representatives of the Member States and chaired by a representative of the Commission (Article 9), the competence of this Committee to be consulted for clarification of the requirements of the annexes and on standards for electronic signature products (Article 10), the notification obligation of the Member states concerning voluntary national accreditation schemes (Article 11), reviewing and implementation rules (Articles 12-15).

Relevance to the Health Telematics Sector

The Directive on a common framework for electronic signatures will, once adopted by the Council, oblige the European Member States to adapt their national legislation. Member states with existing national rules concerning electronic signatures, such as Germany and Italy, may have to amend those elements not compliant with the Directive. Other Member states will be urged to adopt a legislative framework which is in coherence with the contents of the Directive.

From an optimistic viewpoint the national implementation of the Directive may be expected by the end of the year 2000.[21] A more realistic expectation would, however, be the end of 2002.

The influence of the Directive on the Health Telematics sector is likely to be substantial, in both positive and negative terms.

Advantages

- **Political awareness and Users confidence**

An important advantage of the Directive is that it will create awareness amongst the policy makers on both a national and a supranational level (Tab.3). Policy makers will be obliged to take an interest in the issues invoked by the Directive and to draft related legislation. The Health Telematics sector should certainly benefit from this general attention and "jump on the moving train".

Users, both from the professional and the consumer market, will also become more confident in operating electronic signature technologies for everyday day purposes. The step towards the introduction of the same technologies in the Health Telematics sector may therefore come more easily.

- **Electronic signature standards**

The Directive encourages the use of electronic signature technical standards (Article 3.3) and the standardisation of new applications and functionalities. The DG III "European Electronic Signature Standards Initiative" (EESSI) which was launched in February 1999, is expected to give an overview of the technical standards which are

21 The Directive is expected to be adopted by the Telecommunications Council in May 1999, and will entry into force twenty days after publication in the Official Journal. Member States should comply not later than 18 months after entry into force of the directive.

available to meet the requirements of the Directive and of the gaps which still need to be plugged.

The health care sector can benefit from this standardisation process and incorporate the general standards by reference if appropriate. Especially the applicable or future standards for 'advanced electronic signature' and for the fulfilment of the annexes of the directive should be envisaged.

- **General acceptance of electronic signatures for legal purposes**

Electronic signatures may not be denied legal effect solely on the grounds that they are in electronic form. This general legal acceptance of electronic signatures will certainly boost the application of signing electronically. Moreover, Article 5.1 of the Directive requires European Member States to ensure that advanced electronic signatures, based on a qualified certificate and created by a secure creation device are equivalent to hand-written signatures as to their legal effects, and are admissible as evidence in legal proceedings."

Confidence in the legal effects of an electronic signature will also encourage the introduction of electronic signatures in the health care sector. Furthermore, if an 'advanced' electronic signatures is used in the health care sector, legal effects will automatically be granted for it.

However, it should be mentioned that this would only be the case as long as specific health care legislation does not explicitly prescribe the use of hand-written signatures and paper documents (see below, disadvantages).

- **Common market for certification service providers**

Via the Directive a common market for certification service providers will be established (Article 4), encouraging the use of trustworthy certification procedures and signature products. The market-driven approach of the Directive promoting the establishment of certification services deliberately fulfilling a minimum of organisational, procedural and technical requirements (Annex II of the Directive) together with the establishment of appropriate supervisory systems (Article 3.2bis) will certainly raise the security level of certification services to an acceptable level for the Health Telematics sector.

- **Secure cross-border communication by mutual recognition**

Certificates and electronic signatures, as well as certification services will be acceptable throughout the European Union allowing for a secure cross-border information flow without compromising legal effects. From a Health Telematics perspective the current legal and practical obstacles refraining the introduction of a pan-European data interchange may more easily be resolved.

Tab. 3: The relation between technical security and legal certainty. The current situation is on or even below the lowest level in member countries of the EU. The EU directive addresses the medium level.

Level of technical security	Level of legal certainty	
Time stamping, message format, key-length, ...	Informal enhancement of legal certainty	**Extra technical requirements to enhance technical security but not necessary from a legal perspective**
Advanced electronic signature with qualified certificate created by secure signature creation device (art. 2.1bis, 2.3bis, 2.5 Annex I, II, III)	Same legal effect as hand-written signature (art.5.1)	**Minimum technical level for legal equivalency with hand-written signature**
Electronic signature (art. 2.1)	Cannot be denied legal effect	**Minimum technical level for legal value**

Disadvantages

- **Minimum security level**

The Directive introduces a (voluntary) minimum level of technical security for electronic signature products, certificates and related services, and consequently, for electronic signatures. The specificity of the health care sector may, however, urge for a higher level of technical security. Hence, an important question is whether this sector needs more stringent security than the minimal technical security requirements. If so, this would mean that a new legal framework with additional requirements for the health care sector may have to be put in place. There is, however, a risk that policy makers, assuming a common level of security has already established by the Directive, are not interested in drawing up new rules. An important task would be to convince policy makers that while the minimum technical requirements are indeed a step in the good direction, these requirements are not secure enough for the health care sector.

- **Specific health care legislation**

Specific health care legislation in the Member states may still prohibit the use of electronic signatures. The Directive explicitly does not cover aspects related to legal obligations where there are form requirements prescribed by national or Community law (Article 1). Furthermore, Article 3.4 of the Directive states that Member states may make the use of electronic signatures in the public sector subject to possible additional requirements.

In most of the Member States the health care sector is part of the public sector, or at least governed by public law. Therefore, there may still be a risk that in some Member states, electronic health care documents accepted in other Member states, will not receive the same legal value, or will not be accepted at all.

- **Directive limited to electronic signatures**

It should be noted that the Directive limits itself to the acceptance of electronic signatures only. It does not mention the use of electronic documents and certainly does not aim at providing legal equivalency for electronic documents. Hence, there is a risk that national legislation will only be amended to provide legal recognition for electronic signatures while other paper-related legal obligations remain in force, such as for example, an obligation to record information in paper form or to send that information by registered mail. The Directive on Electronic Commerce may, however, resolve this concern.

1.3.2. Draft Directive on Certain Legal Aspects of Electronic Commerce

History of the Proposal

The European Commission published a Proposal for a European Parliament and Council Directive on certain legal aspects of electronic commerce in the internal market. The underlying proposal, also based on the orientations set out in the April 1997 Communication from the European Commission "A European Initiative in Electronic Commerce"[22], was submitted by the Commission on 23 December 1998.[23]

---

22 European Commission, Communication to the European Parliament, the Council, the Economic and Social Committee and the Committee of the Regions, A European Initiative in Electronic Commerce, 15/04/97, COM(97) 157, par. 51; The complete text of the communication is available at http://www.cordis.lu/esprit/src/ecomcomx.htm .

23 Proposal for a European Parliament And Council Directive on certain legal aspects of electronic commerce in the internal market, COM(1998) 586 final, 98/0325 (COD), O.J. 1999/C 30/04. (see also http://www.ispo.cec.be/Ecommerce/legal.htm

The Commission has also taken into account the opinion of the European Parliament[24] and the opinions of the Committee of the Regions and of the Economic and Social Committee.[25]

The Draft Directive addresses a wide range of issues related to electronic commerce, including the formation of electronic contracts, the liability of online service providers, dispute settlement, and the division of regulatory authority amongst different Member States.[26]

Briefly, the Electronic Commerce Draft Directive can be described as follows: the European internal market is free for the delivery of information society services. Service providers will, for consumer protection and information purposes, be obliged to provide the public with relevant information in an accessible manner.

The first discussions on the draft text within the Working Party on Economic questions (Information Society services) of the European Council started in January 1999. A common position on the contents of the draft directive may be expected before the end of the year 1999.

Three years after the adoption of this Proposal, the Commission is to submit to the European Parliament, the Council and the Economic and Social Committee, a report on the application of this Directive, accompanied by proposals for adapting it to developments in the field of Information Society services.

Contents of the Proposal

The Draft Directive wants to approximate national provisions on Information Society services relating to the internal market arrangements, the establishment of service providers, commercial communications, electronic contracts, the liability of intermediaries, codes of conduct, out-of-court dispute settlements, court actions and co-operation between Member states.

The proposal complements Community law applicable to Information Society services, without prejudice to the existing level of protection for public health and consumer interests.

The executive summary of the proposal addresses the issues to be regulated in the following way:

---

24 Resolution on the communication from the Commission to the Council, the European Parliament, the Economic and Social Committee and the Committee of the Regions on "A European initiative in electronic commerce", A4-0173/98, Resolution of 14 April 1998.

25 Opinion of the Economic and Social Committee on the "Communication from the Commission to the Council, the European Parliament, the Economic and Social Committee and the Committee of the Regions: "A European initiative in electronic commerce", OJ C 19, 21.1.1998, p. 72.

26 The draft directive is based on the articles 57(2), 66 and 100a of the Treaty establishing the European Union. The procedure referred to in Article 189b of the Treaty is being followed.

(1) Establishment of Information Society service providers

The proposal removes the current legal uncertainty surrounding this issue by providing a definition of the place of establishment in line with the principles established by the Treaty and the jurisprudence of the Court of Justice. This is a key element for the proper functioning of the Single Market. In addition, the proposal prohibits special authorisation schemes for Information Society services and sets out some information requirements that providers must fulfil in order to ensure transparency of their activities.

(2) Commercial communications (advertising, direct marketing, etc.)

Commercial communications are an essential part of most electronic commerce services. It is therefore important to clarify and facilitate their use. The proposal thus defines what constitutes a commercial communication and makes it subject to certain transparency requirements to ensure consumer confidence and fair trading. To allow consumers to react more readily to harmful intrusion, the proposal requires that commercial communications by e-mail are clearly identifiable. In addition, for regulated professions (such as lawyers or accountants), the proposal lays down the general principle that commercial communications are permitted provided they respect certain rules of professional ethics. These should be reflected in codes of conduct drawn up by relevant professional associations.

(3) On-line conclusion of contracts

Electronic commerce will not fully develop if the conclusion of on-line contracts is hampered by certain formal and other requirements not adapted to the on-line environment. To this end, Member states shall be obliged to adjust their national legislation. In addition, the proposal removes legal insecurity by clarifying in certain cases the moment of conclusion of the contract, whilst fully respecting contractual freedom.

(4) Liability of intermediaries

To facilitate the flow of electronic commerce activities, there is a recognised need to clarify the responsibility of on-line service providers for transmitting and storing third party information (i.e. when service providers act as “intermediaries”). To eliminate the existing legal uncertainty and to bring coherence to the different approaches emerging at Member state level, the proposal establishes a “mere conduct” exemption and limits service provider’s liability for other “intermediary” activities. A careful balance is sought between the different interests involved in order to stimulate co-operation between different parties thereby reducing the risk of illegal activity on-line.

(5) Implementation

Rather than inventing new rules, the Commission has sought to ensure that existing EU and national legislation is effectively enforced. By strengthening enforcement mechanisms, the development of a genuine Internal Market – based on mutual confidence between Member states - is stimulated. Such strengthening is achieved by encouraging the development of codes of conduct at Community level, by stimulating administrative co-operation between Member states and by facilitating the adoption of effective alternative cross-border dispute resolution systems. For similar reasons the proposal also requires Member states to provide for fast, efficient legal redress appropriate to the on-line environment.

Article 1: scope

The first article defines the scope of the Directive, which is primarily to ensure the free movement of Information Society services within the Internal Market. However, the Directive states that this free movement of services shall not prejudice the existing level of protection for public health and consumer interests.

Article 2: definitions

Article 2 provides a few definitions. The entire Directive is built up around a few important terms: "*Information Society services*", "*service provider*", "*recipient of the service*", and "*commercial communications*".

An "*Information Society service*" is any service which is normally provided for remuneration, at a distance, by electronic means and at the individual request of a recipient of services. For the purpose of this definition: "at a distance" means that the service is provided without the parties being simultaneously present; "by electronic means" means that a service is sent initially and received at its destination by means of electronic equipment for the processing and storage of data, and entirely transmitted, conveyed and received by wire, by radio, by optical means or by other electromagnetic means; and "at the individual request of a recipient of services" means a service provided through the transmission of data on individual request.[27]

A "*service provider*" is any natural or legal person providing such an Information Society service. An "*established service provider*" is a service provider who effectively pursues an economic activity using a fixed establishment for an indeterminate duration. Important is that the presence and use of the technical means and technologies required to provide the service do not constitute an establishment of the provider.[28]

The "*recipient of the service*" is any natural or legal person who, for professional ends or otherwise, uses an Information Society service. This would be in particular for the

---

27 This definition was taken from Article 1(2) of Directive 98/34/EC, OJ L 204, 21.7.1998, p. 37, as amended by Directive 98/48/EC; OJ L 217, 5.8.1998, p. 18.

28 Thus, the following, for example, do not amount to an establishment on the territory of a Member State: the location of the technology used, e.g. the hosting of web pages or of a site; the ability to access an internet site in a Member State or the fact that a service provider established in another Member State offers services targeted at the territory of another Member State.

purposes of seeking information or making it accessible; "*Commercial communications*" are any form of communication designed to promote the goods, services or image of a company, organisation or person pursuing a commercial, industrial or craft activity or exercising a liberal profession.[29]

Article 3: internal market

Article 3 contains the Internal Market principle requiring the Member state in which the service provider is established to ensure that his activities comply with the national law of the country (country of origin principle) and, furthermore, that no Member State may restrict the freedom to provide Information Society services from another Member State.[30]

This 'country of origin'-principle will clarify the current uncertainty about which national legal rules should be applicable in an electronic environment. It should be noted, however, that the existing 1980 Rome Convention on applicable law for contractual obligations and the 1968 Brussels Convention on judicial competence continue to apply.

Articles 4 and 5: establishment and information requirements

Article 4 gives effect to the principle of freedom to provide services by facilitating access to the supply of services on the Internet by asking Member states not to introduce any requirement of prior authorisation. This principle is, however, only limited to requirements related to information society services: requirements for access to activities which are not specific to Information Society services continue to be applicable. Thus, for example, if legislation requires professional qualifications or authorisation by a professional body or authorisation to carry on the activities of a travel agency, it will continue to apply in full to any operator wishing to carry on such activities on the Internet.

Article 5 contains a few rules related to information to be provided by the Information Society service provider, such as the name of the service provider and the address where the service provider is established. This information should be easily accessible, in a direct and permanent manner to the recipients and competent authorities.[31]

As concerns the regulated professions, such as *health professionals*, specific information should also be provided related to any professional body or similar institution with which the service provider is registered. Also the professional title granted in the Member state of establishment, the applicable professional rules in the Member state of establishment and the Member states in which the Information Society services are regularly provided, should be made publicly available.

---

29 The following do not as such constitute commercial communications: information allowing direct access to the activity of the company, organisation or person, in particular a domain name or an electronic-mail address, communications relating to the goods, services or image of the company, organisation or person compiled in an independent manner, in particular without financial consideration.

30 However, possible exemptions from the principle are provided for in Article 22(2) and (3).

31 An icon or logo with a hypertext link to a page containing the information which is visible on all the site's pages would, for example, be sufficient to meet this requirement.

Articles 6 to 8: commercial communications

Article 6 refers to the need for transparency in commercial communications. A few obligations for the service provider are introduced, such as the principle that the commercial communication must be clearly identifiable as such. Also promotional offers and promotional competitions shall be clearly identifiable.

Article 7 deals with "*spamming*" practices, i.e. the sending of unsolicited e-mail to consumers or discussion groups. This article requires unsolicited communications to have a specific message on the envelope so that the recipient can instantly identify it as a commercial communication without having to open it.

Article 8 concerns regulated professions wishing to provide an Information Society service. It states that commercial communication is permitted for regulated professions provided it meets the professional rules of conduct applicable to them. Professional associations and bodies are encouraged to establish codes of conduct at Community level to determine the types of information that can be given.

Articles 9 to 11: formation of contracts

Articles 9 to 11 deal with the electronic contracts issues. The main principle of Article 9 is that Member states shall ensure that their legislation allows the conclusions of contracts by electronic means. In particular, they shall ensure that the legal requirements applicable to the contractual process neither prevent the effective use of electronic contracts nor result in such contracts being deprived of legal effect and validity on account of having been concluded electronically.

This means that the Member states have an obligation to succeed, carry out a systematic review of those rules which might prevent, limit or deter the use of electronic contracts and to carry out this review in a qualitative way, i.e. not seek simply to amend the key words in the rules (e.g. "paper") but to identify everything which might in practice prevent the "effective" use of electronic contracts.

Only in a few exceptional cases, such as contracts requiring the involvement of a notary or contracts governed by family law (e.g. marriage), current "paper-based" legislation may remain untouched.

Article 10 refers to the information obligation of service providers related to the formation of the electronic contract.

Article 11 addresses the moment at which the contract is concluded in cases where a consumer is required to give his consent through technological means (e.g. clicking on an icon). The contract is concluded when the recipient of the service has received from the service provider, electronically, an acknowledgement of receipt of the recipient's acceptance, and has confirmed receipt of the acknowledgement of receipt.

The article also requires the service provider to put in place appropriate means for the recipient to be able to identify and correct handling errors.[32]

Articles 11 to 15: liability

Articles 11 to 15 establish limitations on the liability of Information Society service providers, when they act as "intermediaries", as regards illegal acts initiated by others.

Article 12 provides for an exemption from liability related to acts of transmission of information in communication networks where the service provider plays a passive role as a conduit of information for third parties. To benefit from an exemption for potential liability, the provider must respect certain conditions.[33] Article 13 allows for a conditional liability exemption for system caching by service providers. Article 14 sets liability limitation rules for the hosting of information (e.g. the provision of server space for a company's or an individual's web site, for a BBS, a news group, etc.) by a service provider.

Article 15 refers to the principle that service providers may not be obliged to screen or to actively monitor third party content. This general rule, however, does not affect the possibility of a court or law enforcement agency requesting a service provider to monitor in order to prevent or fighting specific illegal activity.

Articles 16 to 21: implementation rules

The Commission proposes to implement the rules of the Directive on a self-regulatory basis. Especially the use of codes of conduct and the out-of-court settlement of disputes are regarded as ideal instruments to implement the electronic commerce rules.

Article 16 encourages the creation of codes of conduct at European level. These codes may be drafted by trade and professional associations or organisations, consumer associations should be involved when they are concerned.

Article 17 obliges Member states to implement an arbitration mechanism for the settlement of legal disputes related to electronic commerce. These mechanisms should be operable in particular by electronic means. In Article 18 the Member States are requested to make the traditional court actions easily accessible for electronic commerce cases. Article 19 obliges the Member States to co-operate by, for example, establishing national contact points which are accessible by electronic means. These electronic means can be specified by the Commission, following Article 20. Article 21 establishes a system for sanctions which can be determined by the Member states. The sanctions they provide for must be effective, proportionate and dissuasive, and must be notified to the Commission.

Article 22: exclusions and derogations

---

32 E.g. the use of confirmation windows allowing the service provider to be able to ensure that the recipient has indeed accepted his offer.

33 The provider does not initiate the transmission, does not select the receiver of the transmission and does not select or modify the information contained in the transmission.

Article 22 contains a list of exclusions and derogations to ensure a degree of flexibility of application of the Directive. The general derogations to the scope of application cover taxation and the areas covered by Directive 95/46/EC on data protection. Certain activities listed in an Annex I are also excluded, such as, the activities of notaries and the representation of a client and defence of his interests before the courts. There are also a few fields of law in relation to which the country of origin principle of Article 3 does not apply.

The specific fields are listed in an Annex 2 containing, for example, the sector of copyright and intellectual rights. Finally, Article 22 in paragraph 3, allows measures to be taken in very specific cases to restrict the freedom to provide Information Society services which would normally be considered incompatible with Article 3(2). These derogations are subject to a series of material and procedural conditions and can only be made for specific purposes such as public security or the protection of public health.

Final provisions

An advisory committee is established with representatives of the Member states and chaired by the representative of the Commission. This Committee advises the Commission on the measures to be taken (Article 23).

Member states shall bring into force the necessary laws, regulations and administrative provisions to comply with this Directive within one year of its entry into force (Article 25). The Directive shall enter into force on the twentieth day following that of its publication in the *Official Journal of the European Communities* (article 26).

Relevance for Health Telematics Sector

On first sight the Electronic Commerce Directive has no immediate relevance for Health Telematics because of its 'commercial' scope. This is, however, not true. The Directive, in its current draft status, applies to:

- ANY service
- provided for remuneration (or financed)
- by electronic means
- irrespective of the legal form under which the provider is operating
- at a distance (i.e. without the parties being simultaneously present)
- at the individual request of a recipient of services

Hence, any health care service meeting these conditions will fall under the scope of the Directive.

Examples:

- An on-line database accessible with health care related information (e.g. electronic cancer registration database) only accessible for medical professionals: the Directive is applicable if a fee has to be paid for accessing the database.
- An Internet search engine meant for medical professionals: the Directive is applicable if a fee has to be paid, but also if the search engine would be financed by commercial banner advertising or sponsors.
- A web-site of a doctor promoting his activities: the Directive is applicable because an on-line commercial communication by businesses or professions to promote their services is an information society service.
- A doctor providing for on-line advice via a web-site or E-mail: the Directive is applicable, because this is a case of telemedicine (which is an on-line service providing medical information or advice).
- An information communication system to exchange electronic patient records between medical professionals: Every medical professional sending, for remuneration, medical information to another medical professional would provide an information society service. In this sense, every medical professional would be a service provider.

It is clear that the rules of the Draft Directive on electronic commerce could have a serious impact on the health care sector, and their national implementation should therefore, carefully be followed and examined.

Advantages

- **The principle of country of origin**

The law of the country in which the service provider is established applies to the delivered services. For the Health Telematics services falling under the scope of the Directive, this would mean that uncertainty as to applicable national legislation would exist no longer. For example, the provision of an on-line database service with health care information by service provider established in Germany accessible for European medical professionals, would fall under German law (note that the European database directive already harmonises the intellectual property rights related to databases).

- **The on-line conclusion of contracts**

The Directive requires the Member states to adapt their national legislation to enhance the legal acceptance of electronic contracts. Member states will have to revoke provisions restricting or prohibiting the use of electronic documents, and to adapt the formal requirements which cannot be met by electronic means (e.g. obligation to put the contract 'in writing', the need for an 'original', etc.). Although the Directive is limited to electronic contracts and not to administrative formalities, which are more common in an

Health Telematics environment, one can expect that the Draft Directive will also encourage the policy makers to reduce form requirements in the administrative sector.

- **Liability of intermediaries**

Common liability schemes for Health Telematics intermediaries would stimulate the implementation of a pan-European ICT infrastructure. The Directive, in fact, puts forward limitations on the liability of intermediaries (Internet access providers, news-group servers, infrastructure providers) as regards illegal acts initiated by others. Intermediaries will be encouraged to work together with Health Telematics because they will not run the risk of incurring liability. This means that, for example, a web-server hosting a web-site or database of a third party containing medical information would not be held liable for wrongful information, copyright infringements or unfair competition.

- **Codes of conduct**

The Directive stimulates the drafting of codes of conduct on a Community level for the implementation of the Directive. Article 8 par.2 especially invites the professional associations and bodies to establish codes of conduct on a Community level.

The emphasis on the need for codes of conduct by the Electronic Commerce Directive will encourage both Health Telematics professionals and the governments to work together to elaborate a common code of conduct which would be applicable throughout the European Union. Codes of conduct should play an important role in the establishment of a secure Health Telematics network. Moreover, instead of waiting for the governmental policy makers to implement the rules of the Directive into national legislation, professional health care bodies could start drafting European Codes of Conduct for the specific implementation in the Health Telematics sector.

- **Out-of-court dispute settlement**

By implementing the Directive, Member states will have to allow effective recourse to these remedies, in particular by electronic means. Currently, prior contractual arrangements are to be made concerning the out-of-court settlement of disputes (mostly written into the interchange agreement). The path of the out-of-court dispute settlement is certainly interesting for the Health Telematics sector in cases where medical liability is not involved. Especially disputes invoked by the use of telematics should be able to profit from the easier arbitration procedure.

Inconveniences

- **Need for specific Health Telematics rules**

 The sector of Health Telematics may need a specific legal framework which is not compatible with the Electronic Commerce Directive. It may now become more difficult to convince policy makers of the need for this special framework, because reference will always be made to the general rules.

- **Divergent legislation between Health Telematics Information Society services and others**

 The risk exists that by differentiating between Information Society service providers, covered by the Directive, and others which are not, a divergent legal framework would be established for Health Telematics. For example, a health care relevant database which is freely accessible would not fall under the scope of the Directive, whereas the same database service, financed by fees, would be regulated by the Directive.

 The distinction made between the services covered and not covered by the Directive may not be appropriate in the health care sector.

1.3.3. The Wassenaar Arrangement and the Dual-use Regulation

Diverse legal instruments exist on national, international and supranational level regulating the use, import and export of cryptography. These legal instruments are in most cases only focused on cryptography for confidentiality purposes and not on cryptography for authentication. The need for regulating cryptography is based on the difficulties law enforcement authorities are confronted with when executing legal interception of encrypted communication or doing search and seizure operations related to encrypted electronic data.

The two most important legal instruments related to the import and export of cryptography on a European level are the Wassenaar Arrangement and the European Dual use of goods regulation.

Description

The **Wassenaar Arrangement on Export Controls for Conventional Arms and Dual-Use Goods and Technologies** was signed by 31 countries in 1996. The arrangement establishes a common export regime for weapons and dual-use goods[34]. Dual-use goods are goods that can be used both for a military and for a civil purpose. Cryptography is considered as such a dual-use good. Software and hardware enabling the encryption of electronic data are not allowed to be exported to third countries (i.e. countries which did not

34 The Wassenaar provisions are not directly applicable: each member state has to implement them in national legislation for them to have effect.

sign the Arrangement) without a license. For mass-market cryptography and public domain cryptography software, though, an exception is made from the rigid rules of the Arrangement. The export of cryptography for personal use (e.g. on a laptop) is also exempted from the Arrangement.

After a revision of the Wassenaar Arrangement in December 1998 the current situation related to export of cryptography is that

- all cryptography products of up to 56 bits key length are free for export,
- mass-market cryptography software and hardware of up to 64 bits key length are free for export,
- the export of products that use encryption to protect intellectual property (such as DVDs) is relaxed,
- export of all other cryptography still requires a license.

The *Regulation No 3381/94 setting up a Community regime for the control of exports of dual-use goods*[35] also regulates the export of dual-use goods, such as cryptography. The general rule of the regulation is that a license is needed for the export of cryptography hardware and software outside of the EU. An exception exists for the export of mass-market and public-domain software. For a transitional period, the Regulation also requires a licence procedure for intra-Community trade of cryptography products. The dual-use regulation is replaced by a new regulation by 1 January 1999, according to the *Proposal for a Council Regulation (EC) setting up a Community regime for the control of exports of dual-use goods and technology*, COM(1998)257final.[36] The main change is that the license for intra-community trade of cryptography technology is replaced by a simple notification.

Relevance for Health Telematics Sector

The need for confidentiality of, for example, electronic patient records urges the health care sector to protect the electronic information by using strong cryptography (e.g. key length of 128 bits). The Health Telematics should be aware that by introducing strong cryptography technology it would not fall under the exceptions of the rules and may have problems to import strong cryptography technology from third countries or to export strong cryptography technology to third countries without a license. The trade of strong cryptography products even within the European Union requires a notification procedure to the national authorities following the rules of the European Dual-use Regulation.

---

35 EU Council Regulation (EC) No. 3381/94 (amended by Regulation (EC) 837/95 of 10 April 1995) and EU Council Decision No. 94/942/CFSP (last amended by Council Decision 98/232/CFSP).
36 Official Journal of 21 December 1998, 98/C 399/01.

1.3.4. Health Telematics Related IDA – programme

The European Commission programme IDA, Interchange of Data between Administrations, aims to enhance the electronic information interchange between national administrations of the European Member States by harmonising the organisational, technical and legal procedures to be followed.[37] The projects covered by the IDA programme vary from electronic tendering procedures to the electronic interchange of customs reports.

From a health care perspective, the IDA funded TESS project, which is situated in the social security sector, may be interesting to investigate.

The TESS project want to develop "Telematic Services for the Co-ordination of European Social Security Schemes".[38]

- ***Description***

The objective of TESS is to simplify and accelerate administrative procedures in order to improve the acquisition of rights and the award and payment of social security benefits for migrant workers.

The TESS programme was launched in 1992. It just finalised its second stage (1994-1998), which aimed at creating a reference system for the implementation of telematic services for the co-ordination of social security systems.

Several results have already been achieved such as the operational exchange of E500 forms for the implementation of Decisions No. 117 and 118 of the Administrative Commission on Social Security for Migrant Workers. In 1997, a "social security glossary of terms" was completed in addition to a set of EDIFACT messages to replace the existing about 80 model forms.[39]

- ***Relevance for the Health Telematics sector***

The know-how built up during the TESS project can be used for enhancing the development of a legally and technically safe information network for health care purposes.

The legal issues investigated during the project and the solutions brought forward involve the legal validity of the electronic message, data protection, modernisation of the legal bases, the need of interchange rules and liability rules.

---

37 Council Decision (EC) No. 95/468 of 6 November 1995 on a Community contribution for telematic interchange of data between administrations in the Community (IDA), OJ. (1995) L 269, 11 November 1995; and the new decision of the Council on 27 November 1998 to fund an IDA II programme.

38 Consolidated version of the Council Regulation (EEC) No. 1408/71 of 14 June 1971 on the application of social security schemes to employed persons, to self-employed persons and to members of their families moving within the Community, OJ [1992] C 325/1, and Consolidated version of Council Regulation (EEC) No. 574/72 of 21 March 1972 laying down the procedure for implementation of Regulation (EEC) No. 1408/71 of 14 June 1971 on the application of social security schemes to employed persons, to self-employed persons and to members of their families moving within the Community, OJ [1992] C 325/96.

39 Responsible administration: DG V, Employment, Industrial Relations and Social Affairs.

1.4. Overview of National Legislative Approaches in the EU Member States [40]

This chapter is mainly based on research up to May 1999. Although national development proceeds and currently gains more momentum, the general principles of the report remain the same. It should be noted that in view of the recently adopted Directive of Electronic Signatures European Member States are amending law which already exists (e. g. Germany) or implement new legislation.

1.4.1. Differing national philosophies

An overview of existing laws or draft laws dealing with digital signatures and electronic documents in the fifteen Member states of the European Union reveals that only a few countries have made any substantial progress on the development of laws, despite the fact that the European Union and UNCITRAL have both produced harmonising draft legislation on the subject. It also shows draft laws to address electronic documents and digital signatures in general, rather than health care in particular.

Some countries have adopted the viewpoint that no new digital signature specific laws need to be enacted since their existing national legal framework deals adequately with documents and signatures in general and is, moreover, flexible and broad enough to cover digital signatures and electronic documents. Others view electronic signatures and digital signatures as completely new concepts, for which new legislation must be enacted.

Among those countries which have enacted legislation or which are developing draft digital signature laws at present, two basic approaches seem to have evolved:

- to only define the most important concepts such as "electronic document"; "digital signature" and "trusted third party" and set out regulations governing just their attribution, role and use;
- to define and regulate in detail the use of electronic documents, digital signatures and trusted third parties as well as to define what kinds of acts such a system could be applied to, where and when an agreement is concluded, liabilities as between the parties and so on.

Thanks to the input of the national experts who contributed to the SIREN legal Workshops and other legal activities a comprehensive overview could be made of the

40 Partly taken from the report on the 2nd Legal Workshop on SIREN which was prepared by Ben A. Stanberry for the Physicians Chamber of Lower Saxony in September 1998

different national approaches to digital signatures and electronic adopted by the Member states of the European Union.

1.4.2. Details on Countries

Austria

A draft electronic signature law is presently under way. Some time ago, the Prime Minister's Office had sent out a set of questions to all of the public administrations and as a consequence the issue of digital signatures is currently discussed in various Austrian ministries.[41]

Three lawyers and a network security expert drafted a preliminary Digital Signatures Act in Autumn 1997, which has greatly influenced the debate on digital signatures in Austria. This unofficial draft is based upon six fundamental principles:

(1) technology-neutrality;
(2) market competition;
(3) different classes of certification for identification and authentication;
(4) continuous updating of certification recommendations;
(5) licensing of certification authorities by an independent body; and
(6) co-ordination with the European Union and other Member States.[42]

Belgium

Responsibility for digital signatures in Belgium lies with the Ministry of Economic Affairs and the Ministry for Social Affairs, and in 1997 a study on digital signature law was carried out by the Interdisciplinary Centre for Law and Information Technology at the University of Leuven for the Office of the Minister of Justice (among others Patrick van Eecke).

During its meeting of 30 May 1997 the Belgian government decided to draft legislation on the Information Society which included the recognition of certification authorities and the use of digital signatures. The proposed law was drafted by the Minister of Economic Affairs in association with the Minister of Justice and approved by the Belgian Federal Council of Ministers.[43] The draft law is compatible with the upcoming European directive.. The regulations establish a voluntary accreditation scheme for certification authorities and

41 Source: Minutes of the European Commission Legal Advisory Board meeting on Electronic Commerce and Computer Crime on 6-7 October 1997.

42 Source: V. Mayer-Schönberger, M. Pilz, Ch. Resier, G. Schmolzer, The Austrian Draft Digital Signatures Act, Computer Law & Security Report, Volume 14, Number 5, 1998.

43 Avant-projet de loi relative à l'activité d'autorites de certification agrées en vue de l'utilisation de signatures digitales - Voorontwerp van wet betreffende de werking van erkende certificatie-autoriteiten met het oog op het gebruik van digitale handtekeningen, approved by the Council of Ministers, 12 June 1998.

appends legal consequences to digital signatures certified by an accredited certification authority. The legal framework allows natural persons as well as legal persons and entities to apply for a certificate.

Legal regulations on provincial or regional levels are not necessary in Belgium. A centralised solution with a public authority (the *Social Security Crossroadsbank*) is intended for the health care sector and, although no health care specific legislation is intended, there is already legislation concerning social security stipulating that electronic documents originating from the social security authorities have the same evidential value as their paper counterparts.[44] Belgian telecommunications law provides for a voluntary prior declaration scheme for service providers.

Denmark

The Danish representative to the SIREN workshop (Henrik Marstrand) reported that there is a discussion in the country about the conflict between law enforcement interests and the requirements to use strong encryption technology in secure Health Telematics.

There are no specific regulations in the health care sector - where closed networks are generally used - regarding either requirements for prescriptions or other health care documents generally. The Danish delegate believed that Denmark will move towards an open network over the coming years and hence decisions will be required on how to protect electronic health care records that are transmitted over these open networks.

Although there is no legislation currently in force governing electronic documents and digital signatures a draft law has been proposed on the secure and efficient use of digital communications. The draft law's underlying rationale is based on the concept that health care and other confidential communications taking place over an open network can only be made legally secure if the recipient is certain of the sender's identity. The proposal suggests public key cryptography as a means of achieving the security of electronic documents and that, in order to certify that these public keys are genuine, there should be one or more certification authorities with a central certification authority established on a semi-public basis. This draft legislation is expected to come into force during 1999. Introducing the legislation at the Copenhagen Hearing, Mrs J. Eis Larsen, Head of Division for IT and Telecommunications Regulation at the Danish Ministry of Research and Information Technology stated that:

> "Our conclusions has been, that there is a need to go through an overall review of all national legislation and regulation through ordinances, in order to analyse whether and

---

44 (K.B. van 22 maart 1993 betreffende de bewijskracht ter zake van de sociale zekerheid, van de door instellingen van sociale zekerheid opgeslagen, bewaarde of weergegeven informatiegevens, B.S., 1 April 1993).

to what extent it will be possible in each individual area to use digital communication. The intention is to combine this general review with framework legislation."[45]

However, given that there are presently no laws preventing the use of cryptography, digital signatures can be legally used. The Danish Contracts Act 1917 sets out the basic principles that will apply to electronic documents and digital signatures. Moreover, under Danish law all evidence is admissible and its strength and reliability can be assessed by a judge. Hence electronic documents signed with digital signatures will be admissible in evidence.[46]

Finland

There is presently no written law or case law in Finland, though the Finnish government is considering legislation which would legally recognise digital signatures. A working group of the Ministry of Justice has carried out a study on digital signatures and looked at the legal situation in other countries but has not yet adopted any official draft.

Issues of debate are likely to be the liability of certification authorities and whether commercial companies and foreign organisations can act as certification authorities.[47] In Finnish law, although over 800 sections deal with signatures, only the Maritime Act 1995 mentions *electronic* signatures. The subsisting point of view in Finland therefore seems to be that:

- laws are not required because the technical environment in which digital signatures are used is safe enough to make signatures totally trustworthy - hence an electronic document with a digital signature will be valid;
- the security "pedigree" of an electronic document signed with a digital signature will depend upon the type of cryptography used; and
- a digital signature has the same legal status as a hand-written one.[48]

The first Finnish pilot projects with electronic identity cards started in the autumn of 1998. These cards will be provided with three key pairs: one for authentication, one for digital signature, and one for encryption purposes. Authentication of the user is achieved at this stage using a PIN code. Later, biometric methods may be piloted. The keys can be used

45 Source: Minutes of European expert hearing on digital signatures and encryption held at Copenhagen, 23-24 April 1998. See http://www.fsk.dk/fsk/div/hearing/ses6/jane.html.
46 See Einersen, E. Electronic contract and evidential law. 1992. IBM, Europay, Mastercard and the Danish company PBS have created a large scale project to provide security for commercial transactions conducting electronic commerce on the Internet. In early April 1997 the new standard called SET (Secure Electronic Transaction) was used in pilot project in Europe for cross-border payments over the World Wide Web.
47 Source: van der Hof, S. and Koops, BJ. Digital signature law survey. (Version 3.1, January 1999). See http://cwis.kub.nl/~frw/people/hof/Ds-lawsu.htm.
48 A project investigating the use of voluntary electronic identity cards was carried out in Finland, see Valtionvarainministeri Liikenneministeri, Sis Asiainministeri, 16.09.96

to electronically sign official documents that require a signature, such as tax forms and social security applications. Transactions, such as the buying and selling of real estate property will, however, still require a notary. The aim is to have most of the "paperwork" produced by the public administration digitally signed by 2001.[49]

France

In France there is no definition of a written signature. A Judge has discretion to decide if information presented in a court of law, including electronic documents with digital signatures, is reliable. In any event a law was passed in 1994 allowing electronic documents to be transmitted between private companies. For the health care sector the appropriate Ordinance was passed in 1996. It stated that a document can be electronic or paper based and a regulation, dated 30 December 1997, formally endorsed the use of electronic documents in the health sector. Two other regulations of 9 April 1998 on health care Professional Cards and Patient Cards define, fairly imprecisely, how digital signatures and electronic documents should be used.

The general feeling among the French participants in the Workshop (François-André Allaert, Jacques Sauret) regarding the potential consequences of the EU Directive on Digital Signatures was that legislation in countries where the use of digital signatures is strictly controlled (e.g., Italy) will need to be widened, but for France it will not cause any changes.

A certification authority already exists: it is a public organisation created in 1993 (GIP-CPS). In September 1998 France Telecom, Gemplus, Matra Hautes Technologies and Verisign launched "Certplus", the national certification authority for the French market. A specific TTP for the health care sector is to be created and will be active within one year. In any case, the EU Directive on Digital Signatures will be useful but technical and organisational problems will remain for France concerning both digital signatures and encryption.

For if smart cards are being used throughout Europe, not all international standards that are used for them are compatible. So to ensure interoperability, low costs and user-friendliness, all the standards of the different sectors have to be compatible (card readers/PC, smart cards/certificates, smart cards/S-MIME, encryption and signature protocols). There is quite a lot to do and industry will only do it if governments, health care professionals and sickness organisations can all agree on the general procedures.

Encryption is probably the biggest question - and one that has to be tackled if we are to create inter-operable systems. In France new legislation - Article 17 of Law on Telecommunications Regulations No. 96-650 of 26 July 1996 has liberalised the use of encryption, making it much simpler for the end user to make use of encryption technology

49 Ibid., at note 7.

and making it possible for suppliers to develop their own range of products.50 A series of recent Decrees and Executive Orders have set out how the law is to be applied and defined the responsibilities of approved TTPs which will store encryption keys in safe custody. Decrees have been made:

- defining the conditions for declarations and authorisations. Signature tools, essential for the development of electronic commerce, can now be used freely. For their supply, only a simple declaration is required which can be processed without any delay and will not require the submission of a technical dossier. For applications which require only a moderate degree of protection, the products can be used freely. Their sales are subject only to a preliminary declaration which is processed within a month, though a technical dossier must be submitted.
- defining the conditions for approval of TTPs. French law provides for total freedom in the use of encryption at the highest level, provided that the keys are managed by a TTP approved by the government on the basis of a dossier allowing an evaluation to be made of the guarantees offered to users.
- setting out, among other things, the contents of a declaration, the format for an application for authorisation, the format for an application for the approval of a TTP and the special measures covering products that don't use TTPs.

This liberalisation of the French regulatory framework has emerged to meet the needs of the market and protect the interests of the many different players concerned. It will also encourage the development of service providers in the field of TTP services.[51]

Germany

On 13 June 1997 the German Digital Signature Law was approved by the German Parliament as Article 3 of a Federal Act establishing the general conditions for information and communication services. Article 3 sets down the general conditions under which digital signatures are deemed secure and forgeries of digital signatures or manipulation of signed data can be reliably ascertained. The law entered into force on 1 August 1997 and while compliance with the law is "voluntary", the German government is open about its intention to create a *de facto* standard for the use of digital signatures.

The German government has issued a Digital Signature Ordinance to implement the digital signature law. The ordinance sets out the requirements and responsibilities for

50 See Journal Officiel of 27 July 1996.

51 Décret no 98-101 du février 1998 définissant les conditions dans lesquelles sont souscrites les déclarations et accordées les autorisations concernant les moyens et presentations de cryptologie et Décret no 98-102 de 24 février 1998 définissant les conditions dans lesquelles sont agréés les organismes gérant pour le compte d'autrui des conventions secrètes de cryptologie.

certification authorities as well as minimum requirements for technical components which are used to create digital signatures. The Ordinance took effect on 1 November 1997.

The first private certification authorities based upon the German digital signature law (the Telecommunications and Post Certification Authority in Mainz will be the national root certification authority) were licensed in 1998. The use of certificates issued by licensed certification authorities will give legal validity to digital signatures under German law. In all instances the private key will be stored on chip cards. However, liability rules (which are present in the EU Directive) are conspicuously absent from the German digital signature laws.

The German law begins with a definitions section (§ 2) which defines terms relevant to compliance with other sections of the law. The other sections of the law refer to procedural and minimal guideline compliance. For example, the definition of digital signature is:

> *"A seal affixed to digital data which is generated by a private signature key and establishes the owner of the signature key and the integrity of the data with the help of an associated public key provided with a signature key certificate of a certification authority or the authority according to § 3 of this Act."*

This definition requires a certificate to be attached to the digital signature and also requires that the certificate be in compliance with other sections of the law. Therefore, a digital signature that has not been issued with a certificate will not be considered legally valid under German law.

In order for a certificate to be valid, German law requires several things to be present. There must be a name or pseudonym attached to the digital signature for identification purposes. There must be a public and private key assigned.

The certificate must contain a serial number. The certificate must describe ways in which the digital signature has been authorised for use. There must be dates of validity including onset and expiration dates. The certificate must also include the name of the certification authority.

The German law requires certification authorities to be licensed by the competent authority of the German government (see § 66 of the Telecommunications Act). They must meet minimal standards and comply with German law at all times. In order to receive licensing from the German government they must show appropriate knowledge and technology in issuing and generating digital signature encryption. They must also certify to the knowledge and proper training of any staff they employ.

The certification authorities licensed under German law are prohibited from gathering information regarding a person from a third party without that person's prior consent. However, they are under an obligation to "reliably establish the identity of persons applying for a certificate". This seems problematic for certification authorities. While the

German law places an obligation upon the certification authority to verify the identity of the applicant, it is restrained from doing so in that it could be forced to take the applicant's word as their own identity. The only way around this problem seems to be to require applicants to approve certification authorities use of third party person verification. This could be done with a driver's license number, address, phone number or suchlike. However, the German law fails to establish how certification authorities will be able to verify identity.

This problem becomes even more apparent by the allowance of the use of pseudonyms in issuing digital signatures. The German law allows a certification authority to issue a digital signature under a pseudonym as long as the certification authority keeps a record of the "real" identity of the person using that pseudonym. In cases of criminal or investigatory matter, the CA is obligated by the German government to turn over the identity of the person using the pseudonym.

Germany's Information and Communication Services Act describes the conditions under which digital signatures and electronic documents are deemed to be secure and incorporates a complex set of regulations setting down organisational requirements. It provides for the organisation of certification authorities by a regulatory authority, and defines key concepts and processes. The German Civil Law needs to be changed to allow electronic documents to be admissible in court with a similar status to hand-written documents and, as a follow up, changes in about 3,000 laws and legal regulations enacted for other reasons but which digital signatures have an impact upon will be necessary.

With regards to technical components, § 14 of the German Digital Signature Law states that during the creation and storage of signature keys and the creation and checking of digital signatures, technical components that have security features that make forgery, falsification and unauthorised use impossible, must be used. This section also sets down generic requirements for technical components that are used to sign and encrypt data and for the maintenance of signature key certificates. These components must be sufficiently examined under the state-of-the-art and their fulfilment of the relevant requirements verified by an organisation recognised by the competent Authority of the German government.[52]

Sections § 16 and § 17 of the Digital Signature Ordinance of 7 July 1997 (passed under § 16 of the Digital Signature Law) set down detailed provisions concerning the requirements for technical components and their evaluation. Section § 17(1) states that the evaluation of technical components must be performed under the "Information Technology Systems Evaluation Criteria" (ITSEC). Moreover, the evaluation of components used for creating signature keys or storing private keys (certificate generation) and for components

52 At present the following organisations are recognised under the Digital Signature Ordinance as being competent bodies for the certification of technical components: Bundesamt für Sicherheit in der Informationstechnik, Bonn; debis Systemhaus Information Security Services GmbH, Bonn; TÜV Informationstechnik GmbH, Essen and TÜV Product Service GmbH, München.

that are offered to third parties for use in the course of business must be certified to cover at least the level "E4" and otherwise at least the level "E2".[53] The valuation of security mechanisms must be "high" and the algorithms and applicable parameters must be suitable.

This instance by German Law on the use of the level ITSEC E4 "high" has been met with criticism by the industry, which at a meeting in Bonn on 19 December 1997 (held by the Federal Office for Information Security (BSI) to review the drafts of their technical catalogues for certification authorities) claimed that this level of security was excessive for many of the uses of digital signatures, would hinder cross-border certification and would not gain ground in Europe. For the time being, however, it is expected to remain in force.

Greece

In Greece there are no general or health care specific laws on electronic documents or digital signatures. There is only a provision in the tax law which permits electronic book-keeping. However these electronic files should be printed by the end of each month and they should be submitted to the tax authorities only in paper form. The legal status of electronic documents is unsettled. The Civil Code regulates only the hand-written signature and accordingly a document has evidential value when it carries the hand written signature of the issuer (Article §160 of the Greek Civil Code). There is an exception for mechanical recordings which do not need a signature at all, such as the mechanical signature that appears on bank notes and share certificates (Article §163). However, an electronic document cannot be regarded as a mechanical recording. Moreover, the electronic documents are not admissible evidence according to the Greek Civil Procedure Law if there is a need to prove something that has a value over 1,500 EURO because this is permitted only by documents - unless it is a transaction for which a document is not routinely used, for instance the commercial transactions. It will be necessary to regulate the use of electronic documents if these should be used in the health care sector because this sector uses the written form, for instance you must show a signed letter of referral from a doctor to get cost reimbursement.

Ireland

On 24 June 1998 the Irish Minister of Public Enterprise announced the publication of a Framework for Ireland's policy on cryptography and electronic signatures which will bring about the legal recognition of digital signatures and the establishment of a voluntary certification authority accreditation system. Accredited certification authorities in Ireland will be obliged to implement mutual recognition agreements between each other.[54]

---

53 See GMB1. of August 8, 1992, p. 545 et seq.
54 Ibid., note 7.

On the occasion of the visit of US President Bill Clinton to Dublin in September 1998 a Joint USA-Ireland Communiqué for Electronic Commerce was published which stated that, among other things, unnecessary legal and regulatory barriers to electronic commerce should be eliminated and the emergence of new ones should be prevented. Moreover, where legislative action is deemed necessary, it should not be to the advantage or disadvantage of electronic commerce compared with other forms of commerce.

The statement called for the fostering of mutual cross-border recognition of electronic authentication methods and a non-discriminatory approach to electronic signatures from other countries as a necessary step in the removal of artificial barriers to cross-border commercial transactions.

Italy

Italy was the first European country to create digital signature laws and at present both Italian Houses of Parliament have approved a draft regulation on digital signatures which is expected to be adopted soon.[55] Article § 15(2) of Law 59/97 states that:

- The acts, data and documents created by public agencies and private persons by means of computer based or telematics systems, contracts drawn up by such means, as well as their storage or transmission by means of computer systems, shall be legally valid and relevant for any purpose of law. All the criteria and ways of application of this law will be defined, for public authorities and private persons, with specific regulations, that will be enacted within the next 180 days from the time of coming into force of this law.

This has now taken place with the passing of regulations by Presidential decree on 10 November 1997. Hence the Italian law establishes the equivalence of electronically signed documents to documents in writing and delegates the Government to implement the principle through further sub-regulations. The draft regulation does not provide technical standards with respect to digital signatures but rather sets out the regulatory framework for implementation thereof and clarifies the application of the provisions on electronic documents with respect to the civil law. However, the system of choice of the draft regulation is asymmetric encryption. The technical standards on asymmetric keys adopted the RSA crypto-system.

The draft regulation provides, among other things, for definitions of an electronic document; digital signature; asymmetric key pairs; private key; signature key certificate; biometric key; time stamp and virtual domicile (Article § 1).

---

55 Legge 13.03.1997 n. 59: Delega al Governo per il conferimento di funzioni e compiti alle Regioni ed enti locali, per la riforma della Pubblica Amministrazione e per la semplificazione amministrativa, Art. 15 c.2, GU 17.03.1997, n. 56.

Article § 2 states that an electronic document, its registration on an informatic support and its transmission with telematic instruments is legally valid.

Article 3 states that a decree to follow will describe the technical rules regarding the valid formation, transmission, registration, copying and duplication of electronic documents. These technical rules will be amended every two years to keep them up-to-date with advances in technology. The same decree will also define the technical rules for time stamps and for the surety, integrity and confidentiality of the message.

By Article 4 an electronic document is considered to be a written document with the same evidential value that Article 2712 of the Italian Civil Code gives to mechanical reproductions of signatures.[56] The same status is afforded to copies, extracts and duplicates of the original electronic document provided that they are created observing the regulations.

The Italian law provides for duty of care obligations for the key-holder. Article § 9 states that anyone who causes damage using an asymmetric key pair is liable to pay damages unless he has shown all due diligence in taking precautions against this.

The use of a digital signature at the foot of an electronic document has been given the same status by Article § 10, c. 2 as a hand-written signature and hence can be used to create a binding contract. Contracts that are concluded with informatic instruments and transmitted with telematic instruments are effective if they are signed using a digital signature and Article § 12 states that the transmission of electronic documents with telematic instruments is to be considered as being the same as notification via the conventional mail system. The new Italian laws do not provide any definition of a trusted third party, not does it provide for their regulation. Only Article § 8 mentions certification authorities, defining them as public or private bodies that certify and keep for ten years or more, public signature keys. Certifying authorities that are private entities have to be set up as public limited companies, joint stock companies or joint corporations and their registered capital must be able to meet at least the working capital requirements for authorised banking enterprises.

Legal representatives and administrators of certifying authorities have to meet the requirements of good repute laid down for persons in executive, managerial or auditing positions in banks; assurances must be given that the certifying authority's responsible technical staff and staff charged with carrying out certification procedures are sufficiently knowledgeable and proficient to satisfy the provisions set out in the regulation and the technical rules established by Prime Minister's decree, having regard to the opinion of the

---

56 Article 2712 of the Italian Civil Code states that: "The photographic or cinematographic reproductions, the phonographic registrations and every other mechanical portrayal of facts or things are valid proof of what they represent, if the person against whom they are produced doesn't refuse to acknowledge their conformity with the same facts or acts." According to Article 2702 of the Civil Code and the Supreme Court of Cassation decisions, a judge may deduce the consent of the signatory to the entire contents of a document from the presence of their hand-written signature on a document.

AIPA Authority[57]. Finally, the quality of computer-based processes and products have to meet internationally recognised standards.

The certification process may also be carried out by a certifying authority whose license or authorisation was issued, subject to equivalent requirements, by another member State of the European Union or European Economic Area. The certifying authority must:

- Accurately identify the person applying for certification;
- Issue and publish certificates meeting the requirements to be set out in the decree referred to in Section 3;
- On request of the subscriber, and with the assent of the third party concerned, specify any power of representation or other title relating to the subscriber's profession or office held.
- Meet the technical rules enacted by decree of the President of the Council of Ministers (within 180 days from the entry into force of the regulation);
- Provide exhaustive and clear information to the applicants concerning the certification practice and the technical requirements necessary to obtain certification;
- Comply with provisions concerning the minimal security standards of computer systems and the treatment of personal data, according to Section 15(2) of Law No.675 of 31 December 1996;
- Not accept the deposit of private keys;
- Promptly revoke or suspend certificates in the following circumstances: on request of the subscriber or of the third party of whom the subscriber is an authorised agent; in case the key has been compromised; on decision of an authority; on disclosure of facts limiting the subscriber's capacity or if abuse or forgery is suspected;
- Immediately make public any revocation or suspension of an asymmetric key pair; and if the certification activity is discontinued and records are consequently invalidated or transferred to another certifying authority, immediately notify the AIPA and the subscribers, at least six months in advance.

The electronics records of the public administration, created by means of computer-based systems are considered as original and primary information (Article 18) and in all the electronic files of the public agencies a digital signature can substitute, in accordance with the regulations, a hand-written required signature.

The Italian law on digital signatures and cryptography takes OECD Guidelines into consideration and will eventually lead to the complete integration of electronic documents into the rule of law and generate confidence in the use of information and communication systems.

---

57 A draft text of technical rules can be found on the Italian AIPA web-site once they are formally enacted in March 1999: http:// www.aipa.it.

Luxembourg

Luxembourg has prepared a law on digital signatures. A "project de loi" which was prepared by the Ministry of Economics in co-operation with the Luxembourg banker's association, was intended to be issued in the summer of 1998. In the draft law national and foreign certification authorities will probably be regulated.[58]

A law of 22 December 1996, which modified Article § 1348 of the Civil Code (the law of evidence) now provides for the use of computer records as evidence in litigation, with the same evidential value as the documents they purport to reproduce.

The Netherlands

There are no definitions of hand-written or digital signatures in Dutch law. A description of a (hand-written) signature, electronic signature (biometrics, scanned hand-written signature or encryption) and electronic document is given in a report of the Dutch Ministry of Justice about electronic legal transactions. A definition of a health care document is to be found or derived from the definitions of "medical file" or "medical record" as used in Chapter 7 of the Dutch Civil Code, on medical contracts. This medical record can be on paper or electronic. In February 1998 the Dutch government adopted a policy document titled *Legislation for the Information Highway* which was prepared by the Ministry of Justice.

The document sets out the government's intention to include general experimental provisions in a civil code which will give the court "something to hold onto", as respects the application of civil law on the electronic highway - a trial and error approach which it is hoped will enable the Dutch legal system to keep abreast of security issues in digital technology. In March 1998 a special working group of the Ministry of Justice produced a report which favoured the use of the UNCITRAL model law on electronic commerce: a functional-equivalence approach which requires the electronic document and electronic signature to be functionally equivalent or, in other words, to fulfil the same relevant functions as a paper document and a manual signature. Among these would be the evidential function, the information and communication function and the protection of third parties. Since the publication of the draft European Union Directive on digital signatures, however, it would appear more likely that this will form the basis of any Dutch legislation.

A national Trusted Third Parties project group, under the responsibility of the Ministry of Transport and Communications, has worked out preconditions for TTP services which are set out in a policy document and the Ministry of Economic Affairs has issued an Action Plan on Electronic Commerce. As regards electronic signatures, the Action Plan refers to the aforementioned project on requirements of form.

---

58 Ibid., note 7.

In any event there is a free system of evidence in operation in the Netherlands and there is no barrier in the Dutch Civil Code to the use of digital signatures and, most interestingly, there has been perhaps the only litigation in Europe concerning the use of electronic signatures.

In *Stichting Centraal Orgaan Voorraadvorming Aardolieprodukten* v *International The Netherlands Bank*[59] (known as the *COVA* case) the defendant bank had granted *COVA* a credit facility. All the payment orders had to be sent from *COVA* by telex, adding to each message an identification code derived from a code list supplied by the bank. *COVA* had also entered an agreement of full responsibility for damages resulting from telexes sent from unauthorised persons if these messages contained the right identification code.

One of *COVA's* employees who was not authorised to use the identification code, sent a payment order, with a telex message containing the agreed identification code. He asked the bank to transfer approximately 9 million Dutch Guilders to a Swiss bank account. The defendant bank, assuming the message and identification code to be correct and original, executed the payment.

It was *COVA's* contention that, as a general rule, the owner of an identification code was not bound by the message that contains its code if it had been used by an unauthorised person. However, the Dutch Supreme Court ruled against them, stating that in considering who should bear the risk of misuse of an identification code it was important to bear in mind all of the relevant circumstances. Accordingly, since the unauthorised person was, in this case, an employee of the owner who had easy access to the code, the plaintiff's loss was a result of their own negligence.

However, had the plaintiff exercised all due diligence to ensure the security of such codes (i.e., fulfilled their duty of care) - which was not in the case here - then *COVA* would not have been liable for their own loss.

Dutch regulations do describe the physicians obligation to build and keep medical files on patients and to destroy medical data at a patient's request. This is regulated in Chapter 7 of the Dutch Civil Code, on medical contracts, and in the Dutch Data Protection Act. These regulations contain general rules for the security of personal data. A medical record can be manual or electronic. Only for a medication prescription is a hand-written signature explicitly required. It is still quite uncertain whether a regulation on digital signatures will be drafted in the Netherlands. A possible regulation of digital signatures under national law will probably be adopted to follow the UNCITRAL Model Law on Electronic Commerce or, what is perhaps more likely now, the draft EU Directive. It will probably be a general law and not one that is specific to the health care sector.

---

59 Nederlandse Jurisprudentie 1994, n. 622.

Portugal[60]

The Decreto-Lei, n. 352/86 of 21 October 1986[61] states that telex, facsimile and other modern techniques are legally valid for the conclusion of a contract for transportation. The fifth paragraph of the introduction to this decree states that the legislature wishes to enact new methods of formalising contracts using informatics and telematics systems, thus leaving it open for them to introduce new laws in the future. This decree has now been updated by further legislation in the framework of the CNPDI - *Comissão Nacional de Protecção de dados informatizados* - the National Commission for the Protection of Computerised Personal Data.

The special law 69/98 dated 28 October 1998 regulates personal data processing and privacy protection within the telecommunications sector, transposing the EU Directive (97/66/CE) into Portuguese law. The legal issues are decided under the actual legislation by the CNPDI together with the ICP - *Instituto de Comunicações de Portugal* - in relation to communications and data transmission.

Spain

Spain has prepared a law on electronic signatures which is currently discussed by its parliament. Apart from this initiative, the new Spanish telecommunications law provides, among other things, for freedom of use of encryption software for telecommunications purposes.

Article 52 of the general law on telecommunications No. 11 of 24 April 1998 provides that use of encryption programmes is allowed on the Spanish telecommunications network and specific conditions of use may be established in the implementing regulations.

The Spanish administration can require notification of the encryption algorithms or of the encoding technique by manufacturers, network operators or end-users. Network operators are required by the law to make decoding equipment available to the police forces in a manner to be defined by the implementing regulations.[62]

Article 45, sub-paragraph n. 5 states that any document created with electronic, informatic or telematic instruments for a Public Administration and any copies of such documents must be considered as being original if their authenticity, integrity and preservation is guaranteed.

The Spanish government is developing PKI-based initiatives for the use of digital signatures in communications between citizens and the public administration.[63]

---

60 Personal Communication by Mr. Joaquim Lupi representative of Portuguese industry
61 Diario da Republica de 21 October 1986, pag. 3172 et ss.
62 European Commission Legal Advisory Board News Bulletin, May-June 1998.
63See note 7 supra. See also Baker, S.A. and Hurst, P.R. The Limits of Trust.

It has reported to the SIREN project[64] that, with the exception of experimental use in some private centres, no electronic system of medical records is presently being used with the Spanish health service. Computer applications currently used in hospitals, clinics and other health centres are mostly restricted to financial and administrative affairs and occasionally, in the most advanced centres, to set the appointment for a visit. The use of health cards is very restricted indeed and they are not used to carry clinical information - they are simply used as a form of identification in order to resolve administrative problems.

Sweden

In 1996 a report on Electronic Document Handling was presented by a governmental committee established to study the need for reform of existing laws as a result of fast developments in the area of information technology. It dealt, among other things, with document handling in the public and private sector. The committee suggested that electronic signatures should be considering as being equivalent to traditional signatures as long as they fulfilled the need for verification. In October 1997 the Swedish Cabinet Office Reference group for Cryptographic Issues published the report *Cryptography Policy: Possible Courses of Action for Sweden* as the first step in the development of Swedish national cryptographic policy. With respect to digital signatures the report stated that "in order to facilitate the development of electronic commerce an initial set of rules should be developed for both the usage of digital signatures and the regulation of those institutions that are responsible for the issue of digital signature key certificates."

In February 1998 an Inter-Ministerial Working Group of non-political representatives of several Ministries published a report entitled *Digital Signatures - a technological and legal overview.* The report deals with, amongst other things, requirements of form, evidence law, certification and control of certification authorities, recognition of foreign certification authorities, content and effect of certificates and liability. The report does not represent formal government policy and there are no official written laws or case law on digital signatures as yet.

The tendency in Swedish jurisprudence is to try and resolve the legal questions arising from the use of digital signatures using rules that have already been established for conventional, paper documents:

> „Questions concerning legal difficulties which arise from digital documents and signatures are thereby replaced by the possibility of creating a legally unified regulation of traditional routines and IT-routines. The functions of a paper document are then replicated within the framework of useful applications without the general principles of legal procedure being affected. The attainment of a sufficient level of security has been

64 Personal communication by J. Torres Huertas, Madrid

judged as being primarily a technical problem, with the presuppositions that it should be possible to verify both the contents and the originator."[65]

Hence in Sweden at present there are special regulations regarding health care documents and, though there is a definition of "document" there is no definition of "signature". It is only stated that a document should be signed. An exception from the demand for a signature regarding situations where obstacles exist gives the possibility of electronic usage.

United Kingdom

On 27 April 1998 the Department of Trade and Industry released a statement on secure electronic commerce announcing future governmental policy with respect to encryption and digital signatures. The DTI announced a clear differentiation of policy with respect to digital signatures and encryption.

The UK Government has introduced electronic commerce legislation to license those bodies providing or facilitating the provision of cryptography services. Principally these would be trusted third parties (TTPs), certification authorities and key recovery agents

Such licensing arrangements would be voluntary, as businesses had requested, although it was hoped that organisations providing services to the public would see the benefit of adhering to a high standard and the public confidence that this will bring. Ownership and control of digital signatures would be kept separate. It was intended that licensed certification authorities - conforming to the procedural and technical standards which such licensing will confer - would be in a position to offer certificates to support electronic signatures reliable enough to be recognised as being equivalent to written signatures, an essential ingredient of secure electronic commerce.

It was not envisaged at that time that the Electronic Commerce Bill would contain regulations specific to the health care sector but the Department of Health has recognised that there may be implications for doctors and patients and did hold discussions with the lead department: the Department of Trade and Industry. Medical records and prescriptions are defined in English law but there is no definition of what is a "signature".

The Government's statement proposed that: "Licensed Certification Authorities offering secure electronic signature services will make a significant contribution to electronic commerce in the UK. They will provide trust that the authentication process is reliable (i.e., an owner of an electronic or digital signature certificate is who they say they

65 See Ministry of Justice, Electronic Documents in Administrative Procedures, Business Life and Bulletin Board Systems, Summary of the report by the IT-committee. Stockholm, March 1996 at page 7. The Swedish Post Service has, together with the Nordic Postal Service in Norway, Finland and Denmark, developed a common email service and will introduce new security services for electronic messaging and electronic commerce. It will be once of the first open international security services, known as the Nordic Post Security Service (NPSS).

are) and consumer and business confidence that the signature mechanism employed is robust and secure.

Organisations facilitating encryption services (for example through offering key recovery or providing key management services for confidentiality) will also be encouraged to seek licences. Such bodies can offer sound business benefits to their clients. Increasingly British organisations are recognising the necessity of being able to recover critical data, which their staff may have encrypted, or the text of the messages they have sent to clients. In such circumstances the permanent loss of an encryption key - perhaps because an employee has left - could be very damaging. Licensed service providers that provide encryption services will, therefore, be required to make recovery of keys (or other information protecting the secrecy of the information) possible through suitable storage arrangements.

In developing its policy on encryption, the British Government has naturally given serious consideration to the risk that criminals and terrorists will exploit strong encryption techniques to protect their activities from detection by law enforcement agencies. Encryption might be used to prevent law enforcement agencies from understanding electronic data seized as the result of a search warrant or communications intercepted under a warrant issued by a Secretary of State. This would have particularly serious implications for the fight against serious crime and terrorism.66

In response to these concerns, the Government intends to introduce legislation to enable law enforcement agencies to obtain a warrant for lawful access to information necessary to decrypt the content of communications or stored data (in effect, the encryption key). This does not include cryptographic keys used solely for digital signature purposes. The new powers will apply to those holding such information (whether licensed or not) and to users of encryption products. They will be exercisable only when appropriate authority has been obtained (for example, a judicial warrant for the purpose of a criminal investigation or, in the case of interception of communications, a warrant issued by a Secretary of State) and will be subject to strict controls and safeguards.

The purpose of the proposed powers is solely to maintain the effectiveness of existing legislation in response to new technological developments. The powers apply only to information which itself has been, or is being, obtained under lawful authority. The Home Office will bring forward detailed proposals in due course."

66 For example, during 1996 and 1997, lawful interception of communications played a part - often the crucial part - in operations by police and HM Customs which led to 1,200 arrests; the seizure of nearly 3 tonnes of Class A drugs, and 112 tonnes of other drugs, with a combined street value of over £600 million; the seizure of over £700 million in cash and property; and the seizure of over 450 firearms. During this period, around 2600 interception warrants were issued by the Home Secretary. (In line with the practice of the Interception Commissioner, this figure relates to all warrants issued by the Home Secretary, not just those for the Police and Customs.)

The Electronic Commerce Bill (a "bill" in the UK is called a "draft" elsewhere) was introduced into Parliament. In the Spring of 1998 British Telecom launched a certification authority in the UK and started digital certificate services which are compatible with the Verisign Trust Network (VTN) - a global network of corporate digital certificates which has 1.5 million customers.

A short time later, in June 1998, Barclays Bank launched "Endorse", a smart card based digital signature service which will be used by the Government to enable newly self-employed individuals to register their self-employed status across the Internet. National Westminster Bank, the Post Office and others are also developing trusted third party services but perceive health care data as being a very small sub-set of general smart card use over the next ten years.

2. Methodologies used in the Legal Studies

2.1. Data and Information Collection

2.1.1. Workshops

The existing literature on the subject consists primarily of narrative work- either from the information- or the legal perspective. The SIREN project therefore combined interviewing, surways (similar to delphi-technique), and extensive evaluation of documented related studies or projects.

Two main activities were the organisation and iterative evaluation of two international legal workshops 1996 in Hannover and 1998 in Frankfurt. Details of those are documented in chapter seven of this report. The results of those workshops plus preparatory and related information was validated in many interviews with representatives of national ministries of health and renowned experts. The original material, which includes a list of actions recommended by the participants of the workshop was handed over to the European Commission in two deliverables of the SIREN study.

A lot of actual important information was grouped by country and is presented in this way. However, to be more helpful for a pragmatic or a strategic approach to the matter, results are presented in relation to two relevant scenarios (chapter 3) and mapped into a strategie reference model (chapter 4).

2.1.2. Other Sources of Information

Existing Reports and Analyses

The editors and key authors have been working in the field of interest for many years and could use the material they have collected. Thus this report received much more input than just from the two legal workpackages organised in the SIREN project namely other projects from European Commission and DG XV as well as G 7 interoperability studies. Also national material from several countries was available namely the UK, the Netherlands, Belgium, Germany, Sweden, and France. Many of these sources are documented in Chapter 7 to allow the reader to investigate the matter in more depth if so needed.

UML Approach

Although there are different national concepts dealing with legal regulations on electronic documents, communication, cryptography and digital signatures, it is necessary to define a common basis for these strategies in order to bring together technical and legal aspects and relevant experts. One approach for this can be the description of the so-called "use cases" (using the formal Unified Modelling Language (UML) method). With the help of this tool legal experts can analyse the current legal situation as well as relevant harmonisation and modification of all IT-security-related procedures in the health care sector.[67]

The UML method is a comprehensive and common tool for experts of different sectors. It designs and describes information systems by adopting different views on the system, such as the "use case view", the logical view, the component view, the deployment view and the concurrency view. Only a part of the UML methodology is needed to fulfil the requirements for security enhancements (e.g. use case diagrams). Use cases define a framework for using systems, especially information systems. Starting with a set of basic use case types it is possible to describe concrete scenarios for IT-communication. The specific health care sector description of a security-related use case is often done verbally and then translated to a standardised abstract UML model. Complex scenarios can be created combining only a few defined basic use case types for IT-communication and necessary security procedures. Simple abstract types and scenarios can then fulfil the legal experts' needs for their analysis. Examples for this basic types would be the communication initialisation, access control, information transfer, user authentication, or for a health care application, the creation or transfer of a patient record. This methodology may be very efficient and result oriented and thus appropriate for the interdisciplinary work of health care professionals, IT-security experts and lawyers engaged in legal analyses and solutions.

---

[67] In the EU-project TrustHealth 2 this approach was adopted and developed for the legal analysis of the demonstration sites in Workpackage I under the leadership of B. Blobel (Otto-von-Guericke University, Magdeburg, Germany). First results and an evaluation will be available at the end of 1999.

2.2. Transformation into Results

2.2.1. Analysis of Two Relevant Scenarios Regarding Liability Aspects

From extensive discussions in the G 7 sub-project 6 as well as in TrustHealth 1and in SIREN, it is to be expected that two main scenarios are mostly relevant for the next decade:

- A patient moving to a different region or country needs medical support. The treating health professional contacts the patient's former health care institution which has patient data relevant for the treatment. The resulting communication of health data requires stringent authentication and security measures implemented by both communicating parties.

- A health professional treating a patient in one country requires tele-consultation with health professionals in other countries. In this case, the same requirements for authentication and security are necessary as in the first example. In addition, the legal framework for such consultations has to be defined.

There is general consensus that tele-assistance will also become an important issue during the next decade, but it is as yet not as topical as the first two scenarios described above.

Different legal concepts are discussed and examined as to how these can be addressed within the limited scope of the SIREN legal work package. In view of the substantial amount of published literature on data protection, SIREN focussed on the analysis of the liability aspects. Nine relevant topics were identified in this context:

- Medical liability
- Organisational liability
- Product liability
- Service liability
- Criminal liability
- Contractual liability
- Patient liability
- Patient safety
- Data protection principles

Each heading was examined in relation to the legal impact of both digital signatures and cryptography. Recommendations for immediate or strategic action will also be made. Results are presented in chapter 3.

2.2.2. Derivation of a Reference Model for the Legal Framework

The use of quantitative or semi-quantitative modelling for the analysis of health care problems has specifically been tried in the 1960s. In view of the very optimistic attitude during those days quantitative or semi-quantitative modelling is today a relevant but highly specific tool in many fields of research. In 1972, the Club of Rome published its famous book "The limits of Growth". The underlying mathematical models were computed in the hospital centre of the Hannover Medical School (MHH) in Hannover, Germany. In 1995, one of the collaborators of the working group, B. Hornung, used the same approach in an attempt to model the environment around Health Professional Cards (HPC). In one deliverable of the EUROCARDS Concerted Action, the working group in Marburg described a conceptual model which also contained legal conditions for card implementations. Because of the complexity of the matter the legal regulations within German health care system were taken as an example.

Today, modelling or the development of hierarchical models is only done in highly specialised working groups. The International Sociological Association founded the research committee 51 "Social Cybernetics" during its global meeting in summer 1998, which deals with this questions including legal aspects. The approach of the Marburg working group has not been continued, thus the concept was not developed into a functioning semi-quantitative model mapped into the DEDUC software which was used for the Club of Rome.

In view of the fact that no other models or model concepts are available, several approaches were made in the course of SIREN to finally derive a conceptual model which could improve the establishment of inter-operable legal solutions for health care systems in the European Union. Therefore, it was tried (as recommended after many days of discussions in the G 7 expert round on Health Data Cards/Health Professional Cards) to define concrete everyday situations in an internationally networked health care system and to analyse legal implications.

On the other hand, an attempt was made to adopt a general approach to the field of Health Telematics and its current developments and to derive a model in a top-down approach describing the medical and technical process and its implications for medical documentation. If the results of both approaches can be abstracted in a general way a reference model would exist. In future research that model needs to be validated.

Fig. 2: The reference model is derived by abstraction from the general recommendations from three different methodological approaches: Analysis of real world developments, analysis of medical and technical development trends, and results of expert discussions in two legal workshops.

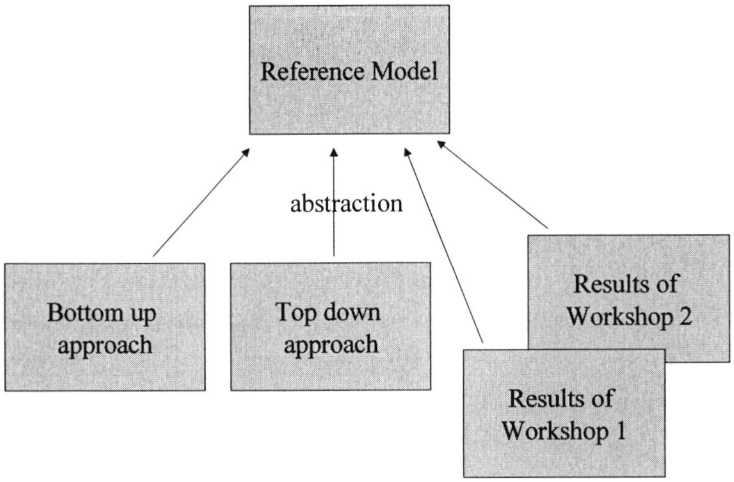

Bottom-up Approach

From Wednesday to Friday, September 23-25, 1998, several SIREN meetings took place in Hannover. Participants in these various meetings were primarily Caroline Laske, Patrick van Eecke, Paul Wenzlaff, and Otto Rienhoff. The results of the workshops were presented to a German national consultation meeting on Friday, 25.9.1998. During the two proceeding days, the following sequence of steps led to a list of legally relevant questions in the field of Health Telematics today:

- Step 1: Discussions at the G 7 Health Data Card Expert Consultation at the Health Cards Conference in Amsterdam in 1997 were again reviewed and slightly extended to two standard cross border work-flows which seemed to be the most likely ones once telematics applications become a real part of the health care services.
- Step 2: A grid was defined which allows systematic description of legal aspects and necessary consequences of actions in relation to different work-flows.
- Step 3: Following some discussion about the relevant legal described here, it was decided to focus the analysis on liability aspects of telematics in health care.

- Step 4: Each of the various work-flows was examined extensively. The results of these discussions were organised into a previously defined documentation grid.
- Step 5: The action list derived from the various work-flows of the grid became a part of a more general list.

Top-down Approach

For a more in-depth understanding of the legal aspects of medical documentation, the question was asked whether there are new demands for the implementation of digital signatures or security systems including cryptography.

For this purpose, the study analysed in a top-down approach the potential effects of global developments for the medical documentation process and for the legal aspects discussed in SIREN

The top-down description of the medical and technical developments follows the main trends common in these fields:

- diagnosis and treatments on the basis of individual molecular biology
- prevention and decentralised care for an ageing multi-cultural population and
- diagnostic and therapeutic procedures supported by knowledge management
- management, micro-devices and virtual reality representations.

However dynamic these developments may appear, there is one stable element: a contract between a patient and a health professional which will be sufficiently documented in accordance with the well developed systematic roof of medical documentation (as it is called in the German context) or medical librarianship (as it is called in the US environment). The results are presented in chapter 4.

3. Liability Reference Model

The results of the different methodological approaches and their relevance will be discussed in the following chapters.

The free movement of services and persons is one pillar of the EU integration project. Its advent has thus a number of repercussions on matters which go beyond the mere economic objectives envisaged by the architects of the Single Market. The free movement of people necessitates, among others, a liberalisation of EU wide health care which together with the technical possibilities offered by telematics and informatics technologies will create innumerable new situations.

The SIREN project has singled out two scenarios which it considers will be most common during the next few years. Point 1 below will consider the situation in relation to mobile patients, seeking (or in need of) health care away from their usual place of residence, either within the same country or in another EU state. In this scenario it is thus a question of sharing patient information between health care providers about a person who is geographically removed from his/her usual place of health care arrangement. This may possibly be undertaken across national borders.

The second scenario under discussion in point 2 below is the increased electronic, digital and multi-media communication between health care professionals with a view to sharing medical expertise, either in form of knowledge-based systems, second medical opinions or telediagnosis. Similarly, to the previous scenario, such communication may take place within one state or across a national border.

Mobile Patients

Patients may seek or be in need of health care away from their usual place of residence, either because circumstances are such that they are unable to return for treatment or because they wish to obtain a second medical opinion in a different location. In either case, it is likely that this will give rise to the need for communication of patient information between the patient's usual health care professional and the one consulted on this specific occasion. The sharing of patient information between colleagues of the medical profession in the course of treatment and diagnosis has been a long established practice and is codified in medical law and codes of good practice. The rule of thumb is that, in the interest and well-being of the patient, information must be shared between health professionals, the emphasis being on *health professional*.

In practice health professionals may be most ready to share patient information within their own health care institution, less ready if it goes beyond their institution and probably most reluctant in relation to foreign colleagues. The basis for this reluctance is three dimensional : psychological, ethical and legal. And the underlying reason is that the further away the communicating parties are from one another, in geographical, social or cultural terms, the least they are prepared to trust each other and thus to exchange their patients' information.

In legal terms, the most contentious issue in this context is the identity, legal status and authentication of the communicating parties. A health professional is only authorised to share patient information with other health professionals, which raises the question of who can be considered a health professional. This can usually be established by reference to national medical law. These may, however, differ between Member states, which potentially raises not only a legal but also an ethical problem for the health professional who is requested to communicate patient information, in particular to a colleague abroad.

Nevertheless, even within the same jurisdiction, health professionals are usually organised into professional bodies which provides their members with the necessary accreditation. Some health related professionals are either not organised in such a manner or are not recognised by national law. This is particularly the case with many para-medical professions (e.g. mid-wives, psycho-therapists etc.) or those active in parallel medicine (e.g. acupuncture, osteopathy, homeopathy etc.). Furthermore, there may be divergence between the professional status of those practising in public health systems and in private institution. Frequently, the latter is governed by less specific and stringent legislation. Again such divergence may create uneasiness among health professionals to communicate with colleagues whose professional credentials are unfamiliar to them.

In conclusion it can be said that for effective patient mobility and the necessary transfer of patient information there is the need for EU-wide recognition of professional status, of harmonised codes of good practice (in particular in relation to health care records), of authentication procedures, as well as the possibility for widely ascertainable verification of authentication. While digital signature and encryption technologies may offer an appropriate means to deal with identification and authentication issues this is, however, of limited utility if legislation or regulation do not establish the point of reference which identification /authentication must guarantee.

There is a further aspect to the reticence health professionals may experience when having to share patient information with colleagues/health care system unfamiliar to them. It concerns the fear that once health professional A has communicated data to colleague B, the former no longer has any control over the data. This raises the long and heatily debated question of who can be considered the owner of a set of data. The concept of ownership is perhaps somewhat inappropriate. The notions of intellectual property right and that of actual control/responsibility are probably more relevant to health care, medical records and patient information. Thus, while health professional A operates within a system with established rules well known to him/her, communicating patient data to colleague B, whose professional accreditation, health care system, code of conduct etc. may be unfamiliar to A could result in reluctance to undertake such exchanges of patient information. What will happen to the hence exclusive control of health professional A exercised over the patient information? According to what rules will B allow patient access to his data? Legal, ethical and medical issues of this kind have been raised ever since health professionals have communicated with each other about particular patients. The implementation of technologies such as informatics and telematics merely intensifies the debate since they provide the means for communication on a large scale.

While legal harmonisation in the question of mutual recognition of professional qualifications and accreditation is a pre-requisite for the effective application of the sharing-patient -information-among-health-professionals rule, the adoption of a code of practice on how to manage and control the actual exchange of patient information would allow for some of the ethical and perhaps psychological obstacles to the sharing of such information in the context of mobile patients.

Sharing Medical Expertise

Health professionals consulting colleagues for second opinions or other sources of information during the course of their work is a long-established practice. Since the advent of informatics and telematics technology, the means and possibilities of such consultations have become widely available and increasingly sophisticated. The scenario under discussion in this chapter restrict itself to health professionals communicating via electronic and digital means for the purposes of establishing a diagnosis. The danger that the liability of the communicating parties may become blurred in such telemedicine / telediagnosis scenarios is a real one, mainly due to the potential volatility of the data in question. Thus the key is transparency and accountability of the entire communication so as to allow retroactively for the form, content and results of given process to be ascertained.

It has been suggested[68],[69] that the liability issues in telemedicine scenarios may be dealt with by means of a contract concluded between the communicating parties, clearly setting out the liabilities incurred by each party. This is altogether not a fortunate solution, in particular in view of the fact that in common law legal traditions third parties would not be able to enforce the terms of such contracts, typically concluded between the two health professionals. In this case, patients whose health is the subject of the teleconsultation are thus excluded from the terms of such contracts. Nevertheless, the contract solution is handy in the absence of any appropriate regulation, codes of conduct or case law that may provide

---

68 François-André Allaert and Dusserre L., Legal Requirements for Tele-Assistance and Tele-Medicine, MEDINFO 95, Proceedings, Greene R.A et al. (eds.), p. 159
69 François-André Allaert and Dusserre L., Tele-expertise: Users' and Suppliers' Liability, Medical Informatics Europe '96, Brender J. et al. (eds), p. 957

guidance as to questions of liability. It is indeed advisable for communicating parties to conclude such contracts specifying, among others, the duties, responsibilities and liabilities of the parties concerned. Such a contract may also provide the opportunity to address questions such as medical confidentiality, data protection, security, access and transmission policies, audit trails and the observance of any other specific procedures/codes of good practice. The contract can further stipulate what would constitute evidence in case of a legal action.

Definition of Liability

Liability is the legal term to determine the effects of wrongdoing of a legal subject.

All European Member States have their own liability schemes and procedures. All of them are, however, based on the following principles:

- Someone can only be held liable if a legal rule (legislation, case law) exists on which the action can be based;
- There should be damages;
- There should be a cause (fault, negligence);
- There should be a link between the damages and the cause (causal link).

These conditions go for all types of civil liability (contractual liability, extra-contractual (torts-delict)). For criminal liability the rule of thumb is that any breach of criminal law automatically gives rise to liability independent of the issue of damages.

Medical Liability

A health care professional faces liability for actions related to his/her medical status, such as the wrongful execution of medical services causing personal injuries, or the breach of confidentiality. Medical liability could lead to damages or to professional repercussions (e.g. suspension by the professional organisation). The introduction of Health Telematics may expose the health care professional to new forms of medical liability. The shift from traditional paper health care records to electronic patient records, for example, could invoke new questions of medical liability. Digital signatures and encryption may help to find a structured balance between the application of Health Telematics and medical liability.

Organisational Liability

Health care organisations, such as hospitals, are responsible for the introduction of Health Telematics. The malfunctioning of the information and communication systems may cause liability towards the users (e.g. doctor) and consumers (e.g. patient) of the new technologies. To minimise the risk of malfunction causing organisation liability new security procedures and related actions may need to be introduced involving the use of digital signatures and encryption.

Product Liability

Faulty products causing damages could lead to product liability for the producer of the product. The current product liability rules may, however, not cover the specificities of Health Telematics, hindering an effective attribution of damages. The current status of 'product' liability for software is, for example, uncertain and could lead to a reluctance to introduce Health Telematics.

Service Liability

Every service provider causing damages during the execution of the service contract, may be held liable. The introduction of Health Telematics may, however, invoke new forms of damages for which the current liability schemes may not be sufficient.

Criminal Liability

The breach of national criminal legislation would invoke criminal liability. Countries in which no criminal legislation exists relating to harmful activities in an electronic environment, could hinder the deployment of Health Telematics. Digital signatures and encryption could, however, play a preventive role.

Contractual Liability

New types of contracts, and new ways of concluding contracts may question the traditional contractual liability.

Patient Liability

A specific liability for the patient in his relationship to the physician is currently non-existent because of the patient's minimal role. The introduction of Health Telematics may put the patient on a more active level, extending his liability.

Patient Safety

Health Telematics may cause new risks for the infringements of patient's rights. The patient safety should be a main element in introducing new technologies.

The issue of liability has been taken for demonstration of the impact of digital signatures in health care, because it is expected that telemedicine will improve service for patients substantially and will create a market which may create liability problems.

The following tables describe a "shift" by use of Health Telematics and interpret the shift in relation to major security techniques, the general and legal situation today and recommend immediate and strategic actions.

Using the term "shift" shall indicate a major change introduced through Health Telematics in many fields of health care. It shall not indicate that liability issues rise in the existing systems but that they rise when a third element (see footnote) is introduced in the patient doctor relationship and when we look into international health services.

Tab. 4: Impact of Health Telematics Security technology on legal development regarding:

Medical liability (Regarding Patient - Health Professional Relationship)

Shift by use of Health Telematics	A third element appears in the patient-health professional relationship, e.g. other professionals (e.g. computer specialists), computer or internet info robot. These dilute the mutual and direct patient-health professional relationship.
How can it be dealt with through digital signatures and cryptography	Digital signature allows for the third element to remain under the control of the health care professional. No specific use of cryptography
Situation today and impact of EU main legal instruments/initiatives	*General:* In view of the fact that this is not regulated, telematics technology increasingly becomes and remains a third element => mistrust *Impact of EU main legal instruments/initiatives*: COM(1998)297 (Directive on Digital Signatures) COM(1998)586 (Draft Directive on Electronic Commerce)
Immediate action and strategic necessities	*Immediate action*: Awareness raising *Strategic necessities* : Adoption of Code of Practice as recommended by COM(1998)586 as well as adoption of electronic signature procedures as laid down in COM(1998)297,

Tab. 5: Impact of Health Telematics Security technology on legal development regarding:

Medical liability (Regarding Health Care Record)

Shift by use of Health Telematics	Health care record changes to electronic patient record (EPR) as means of medical documentation
How can it be dealt with through digital signatures and cryptography	Health care record = volatile => need for digital signature; in view of the very different nature of the health care records, digital signature allows for greater transparency, in particular in relation to the origin of information No specific use of cryptography
Situation today and impact of EU main legal instruments/initiatives	*General:* No (quasi) legal regulation; the term health care record is used to describe very different types of records => confusion and different legal concepts are relevant *Impact of EU main legal instruments/initiatives:* 95/46/EC (Protection of the individual with regard to the processing of personal data and the free movement of such data), in particular Art. X (security requirement); 97/66/EC (Processing of personal data and the protection of privacy in the telecommunication sector), R(97)5 (Council of Europe Recommendation on the Protection of Medical Data), (also in particular Art. X (security requirements), COM(1998)297
Immediate action and strategic necessities	*Immediate action* : Use of informatics/telematics technology to allow for increased clarity and transparency *Strategic necessities*: Promotion of secure architectures as required by 95/46/EC, and recommended by R(97)5; Keeping the transmission of the electronic health care record confidential as required by 97/66/EC; Adoption of electronic signature procedures as laid down in COM(1998)297

Tab. 6: Impact of Health Telematics Security technology on legal development regarding:

Medical liability (Regarding Confidentiality)

Shift by use of Health Telematics	Confidentiality: in view of the greater accessibility of information and the possibility to analyse merged data sets, potential economic exploitation becomes a real threat
How can it be dealt with through digital signatures and cryptography	Digital signature technology allows to prove the origin of data and thus to trace the origin of breaches, even retroactively; it therefore increases confidentiality
Situation today and impact of EU main legal instruments/initiatives	*General:* Electronic documents are increasingly handled without appropriate possibilities to check their authenticity and integrity and to guarantee confidentiality *Impact of EU main legal instruments/initiatives*: 95/46/EC, 97/66/EC, R(97)5, COM(1998)297, OECD (Recommendation for Cryptography Policy), Wassenaar (Arrangement on Export Control)
Immediate action and strategic necessities	*Immediate action*: Enforcement of existing regulations which require all personal data to be authenticated => in digital environment use of digital signature should be mandatory *Strategic necessities*: Respecting the confidentiality of communication following the rules of 95/46/EC, 97/66/EC and R(97)5; Adoption of electronic signature procedures as laid down in COM(1998)297; The use of appropriate confidentiality tool such as encryption can be promoted by the OECD recommendation, and hindered by the Wassenaar arrangement and the EU Dual-goods regulation

Tab. 7: Impact of Health Telematics Security technology on legal development regarding:

Medical liability (Regarding Use of Health Telematics)

Shift by use of Health Telematics	Use/non-use of this type of technology: increased availability of medical information offers advantages to the individual as well as to health care at large => the use of Health Telematics will become increasingly a part of the state-of-the-art
How can it be dealt with through digital signatures and cryptography	Digital signature allows for conventional processes to be translated into the digital environment in an equivalent way and may thus make Health Telematics more widely used; a securer environment will be created by digital signature and encryption
Situation today and impact of EU main legal instruments/initiatives	*General*: In view of the fact that such technology is not being used there is an increasingly unregulated use of medical documents *Impact of EU main legal instruments/initiatives*: COM(1998)297, COM(1998)586, 95/62/EC (Directive on the application of open network provision to voice telephony), 98/10/EC (Directive on the application of open network provision to voice telephony and on universal service for telecommunications), OECD (Recommendation for Cryptography Policy), Wassenaar (Arrangement on Export Control)
Immediate action and strategic necessities	*Immediate action*: All (quasi)-legal regulation discriminating against the use of digital documents should be repealed; all electronic documents must through the implementation of security measures be given similar status to those in the conventional environment *Strategic necessities*: Adoption of electronic signature procedures as laid down in COM(1998)297; General acceptability of the use of telematics because of COM(1998)586, 95/62/EC and 98/10/EC; The use of appropriate confidentiality tool such as encryption can be promoted by the OECD recommendation, and hindered by the Wassenaar arrangement and the EU Dual-goods regulation

Tab. 8: Impact of Health Telematics Security technology on legal development regarding:

Medical liability (Regarding Authenticity/ Identification)

Shift by use of Health Telematics	Authenticity/identification: increased communication and the missing ability to identify the communication partner through human means provides less control for the health care professional
How can it be dealt with through digital signatures and cryptography	Digital signatures, if appropriately used, guarantee authentication and communication partner identification
Situation today and impact of EU main legal instruments/initiatives	*General*: See above *Impact of EU main legal instruments/initiatives*: 95/46/EC, 97/66/EC, COM(1998)297
Immediate action and strategic necessities	*Immediate action*: Digital signature technology is in itself insufficient, there is the need to recognise such technology through certification *Strategic necessities*: Certification should be co-ordinated on international level and should take into account the specificities of the health care sector; Certification authorities within health care have to be a part of a health care specific hierarchical certification system or be cross-certified by other certification authorities in the health care system Certification procedures following 95/46/EC and 97/66/EC, and as suggested by COM(1998)297

Tab. 9: Impact of Health Telematics Security technology on legal development regarding:

Organisational liability (IT Security Policy)

Shift by use of Health Telematics	IT security policy: Because of Health Telematics there is a need for an adapted security policy
How can it be dealt with through digital signatures and cryptography	Digital signature technology and encryption are the cornerstones in effective IT security policies for health care organisations
Situation today and impact of EU main legal instruments/initiatives	*General*: Digital signature and encryption are not yet widely used as part of the IT security policy *Impact of EU main legal instruments/initiatives*: 95/46/EC, R(97)7)5; COM (1998)585 (Green Paper on Access to Public Sector Information), 21/12/1998 (EU Action Plan Promoting Safer Use of Internet), OECD (Recommendation for Cryptography Policy), Wassenaar (Arrangement on Export Control), and 3381/94/EC
Immediate action and strategic necessities	*Immediate action*: IT security policies should be mandatory for health care organisations using appropriate IT; therefore allocation of sufficient resources is needed *Strategic necessities*: Encourage IT security training and awareness programmes for health care managers; Development of IT security policies as laid down in 95/46/EC and R(97)5; Adoption of recommendations of the EU Action Plan on safer use of the Internet The use of appropriate confidentiality tool such as encryption can be promoted by the OECD Recommendation, and hindered by the Wassenaar arrangement and the EU Dual-goods regulation

Tab. 10: Impact of Health Telematics Security technology on legal development regarding:

Organisational liability (IT Security - Staff Performance)

Shift by use of Health Telematics	Appropriate performance by staff in a secure IT environment
How can it be dealt with through digital signatures and cryptography	Not specifically helpful
Situation today and impact of EU main legal instruments/initiatives	*General*: Risk of non-appropriate performance as training is still ineffectively carried out (not requested by law) *Impact of EU main legal instruments/initiatives*: No legislation on European level; national labour law, health law, hospital legislation,... involved
Immediate action and strategic necessities	*Immediate action*: Mandatory training and awareness raising for security risks in the IT environment and the importance of effective use of digital signature technology; also essential is appropriate training of staff in the use of such technology *Strategic necessities*: Incorporation of these principles into the auditing manuals for health care organisations

Tab. 11: Impact of Health Telematics Security technology on legal development regarding:

Organisational liability (IT Security - Implementation)

Shift by use of Health Telematics	Proper implementation, use and servicing of IT technology, e.g. certification authorities (CA) services.
How can it be dealt with through digital signatures and cryptography	Not specifically helpful
Situation today and impact of EU main legal instruments/initiatives	*General*: Risk of improper implementation could give rise to organisational liability *Impact of EU main legal instruments/initiatives*: COM(1998)297
Immediate action and strategic necessities	*Immediate action*: Specifically for the implementation of a certification authorities service, the implementation of the guidelines as laid down in COM(1998)297 will minimise organisational liability

Tab. 12: Impact of Health Telematics Security technology on legal development regarding:

Product liability

Shift by use of Health Telematics	Increasing number of medical tools contain informatics and telematics components; for those which fall either under conventional product liability law or which are covered by medical devices legislation, the issue of liability has been addressed, for the remaining tools the product liability issue is unclear
How can it be dealt with through digital signatures and cryptography	Digital signatures are not relevant to this liability case, except in some cases, such as aggregated products: Digital signature procedures for software tools may help to trace the various components *Cryptography*: Not relevant
Situation today and impact of EU main legal instruments/initiatives	*General*: unsolved *Impact of EU main legal instruments/initiatives*: 92/59/EEC (Directive on General Product Safety) and 93/42/EEC (Directive on Medical Devices) of limited application
Immediate action and strategic necessities	*Immediate action*: Digital signature and cryptography software have to be regulated in a way that does not raise new liability issues *Strategic necessities*: Further research has to address the unsolved question of software liability

Tab. 13: Impact of Health Telematics Security technology on legal development regarding:

Service liability

Shift by use of Health Telematics	New technologies give rise to a wide range of new kinds of services, in particular health care related services over a distance
How can it be dealt with through digital signatures and cryptography	Digital signature technology in the context of authentication and data security allows for better assessment of contentious liability questions Cryptography in the context of safeguarding the confidentiality of sensitive medical data
Situation today and impact of EU main legal instruments/initiatives	*General*: At present there are various national and sub-national regulations, as well as specific regulations in professional ordinances dealing with the provision of health care to a patient over a distance, some of which outlaw such practices (e.g. Germany), in particular in a transborder scenario (i.e. mutual recognition of professional accreditation) *Impact of EU main legal instruments/initiatives*: COM(1998)586
Immediate action and strategic necessities	*Immediate action*: Reassessment of regulations in this area allowing patient-oriented reliable telemedicine services *Strategic necessities*: The few health care related services will certainly be seen as an Information Society service covered by COM(1998)586

Tab. 14: Impact of Health Telematics Security technology on legal development regarding:

Criminal liability

Shift by use of Health Telematics	As such there is no actual shift in liability under criminal law, however high efficiencyin the communication of diagnostic results may lead to greater risks and potential damages in case of lost/manipulated data (hacking and data fraud, etc.)
How can it be dealt with through digital signatures and cryptography	Application of digital signature may reduce the risk of fraud and data manipulation by highlighting unauthorised processing. Use of encryption may reduce the risk of unlawful access
Situation today and impact of EU main legal instruments/initiatives	*Impact of EU main legal instruments/initiatives*: 97/66/EC, R(89)9 (Council of Europe Recommendation on computer-related crime), and R(95)13 (Council of Europe Recommendation concerning problems of criminal procedure law connected with information technology)
Immediate action and strategic necessities	*Immediate action*: All countries should follow-up on the recommendations of the Council of Europe (R(89)9 and R(95)13

Tab. 15: Impact of Health Telematics Security technology on legal development regarding:

Contractual liability (New Type of Contracts)

Shift by use of Health Telematics	In view of the increasing number and complexity of contracts dealing with telemedicine products and services there may be the need for new kinds of contracts dealing with new types of medical business
How can it be dealt with through digital signatures and cryptography	Digital signature can be used as a tool for the conclusion of such contracts, in order to give them maximum legal recognition; Digital signature can become an integral part of such contracts in terms of security management; Encryption can be used as a tool for the conclusion of such contracts, in order to give them maximum legal recognition; Encryption can become an integral part of such contracts in terms of security management
Situation today and impact of EU main legal instruments/initiatives	Such practices can be found in other sectors such as electronic commerce, but are used very little in practice
Immediate action and strategic necessities	*Strategic necessities*: Development of model contract specific to health care with particular emphasis on digital signature, certification authorities, and cryptography

Tab. 16: Impact of Health Telematics Security technology on legal development regarding:

Contractual liability (Online Contracts)

Shift by use of Health Telematics	Online-Telemedicine and other health care-related services may require online contracts
How can it be dealt with through digital signatures and cryptography	Use of digital signature as alternative for hand-written signature Use of encryption for securing confidential contracts
Situation today and impact of EU main legal instruments/initiatives	*General*: Uncertainty about the legal status of digital signature and electronic contract *Impact of EU main legal instruments/initiatives:* COM(1998)297, COM(1998)586
Immediate action and strategic necessities	Legal recognition of digital signature following the requirements of COM(1998)297 and legal recognition of electronic contracts as laid down in COM(1998)586; In specific situations it may be advisable to conclude interchange agreement prior to the service provided

Tab. 17: Impact of Health Telematics Security technology on legal development regarding:

Patient liability

Shift by use of Health Telematics	The fact that patients becomes increasingly active in the decision-making for their health care, including the provision of health data to the health care professional Particularly relevant in the context of teleassistance
How can it be dealt with through digital signatures and cryptography	Digital signatures enable patients to authenticate their part of the process. Digital signature technology enables retroactively to retrace the processes that have been undertaken and may thus provide clarification as to liability in disputes
Situation today and impact of EU main legal instruments/initiatives	Not used
Immediate action and strategic necessities	Further research needed, including the consideration of whether such a development is advisable

Tab. 18: Impact of Health Telematics Security technology on legal development regarding:

Patient safety

Shift by use of Health Telematics	Particularly relevant in the context of teleassistance, radiology, and robotics
How can it be dealt with through digital signatures and cryptography	Digital signature technology enables retroactively to retrace the processes that have been undertaken and may thus provide clarification as to liability in disputes; see product liability above Use of encryption may reduce the risk of fraudulent manipulation and will hence increase patient safety
Situation today and impact of EU main legal instruments/initiatives	*General*: Digital signatures and encryption are not widely used in relation to patient safety *Impact of EU main legal instruments/initiatives*: See above "medical liability"
Immediate action and strategic necessities	Awareness raising

Tab. 19: Impact of Health Telematics Security technology on legal development regarding:

Data protection principles

Shift by use of Health Telematics	New body of law aimed primarily at information technology processing
How can it be dealt with through digital signatures and cryptography	Particularly relevant in the context of data protection principles dealing with access authentication policy; Particularly relevant in the context of data protection principles dealing with confidentiality
Situation today and impact of EU main legal instruments/initiatives	*General*: Today's data protection legislation reflects the technical realities of the 1970s *(example)* *Impact of EU main legal instruments/initiatives*: 95/46/EC, 97/66/EC, R(97)5, OECD (Recommendation for Cryptography Policy), Wassenaar (Arrangement on Export Control), 3381/94/EC
Immediate action and strategic necessities	*Immediate action*: Encouraging the use of digital signatures and cryptography technology in order to implement more effectively the data protection principles; *Strategic necessities*: Respecting the confidentiality of communication following the rules of 95/46/EC, 97/66/EC, and R(97)5; Use of appropriate confidentiality tools such as encryption can be promoted by the OECD Recommendation and hindered by the Wassenaar Arrangement and the EU Dual-Goods Regulation Further research on supportive IT concepts, e.g. personal identity protector

4. Strategic Reference Model

Medical data are usually mapped into medical documents which are entities of related medical data and which due to their characteristies, can be positioned in an n-dimensional document-space. Some basic dimensions of this space are:

- the reality dimension (spanning from virtual data to real data),
- the preciseness dimension (spanning from vague to molecularly defined),
- the identification dimension (spanning from identified to anonymous data),
- the predictive power dimension (spanning from no power to determining power).

Additional dimensions can easily be found. In a given context some are more important than others. Several decades of accumulated knowledge on this issues represents the discipline of medical documentation.

Depending on all types of agreements between communicating parties, medical documents can be defined in a region in this space. In the real world of doctor-patient encounters medical documents were clearly identified, vague in content and conclusion, somehow real and with limited predictive power. For this specific situation legal regulations of different kinds have been derived: e.g. the Hippocratic Oath.

When computer systems emerged in the 1960s, data protection regulations were added to existing national legal regulations, since a new dimension had become relevant in that space: the security of medical documents outside the personal patient-doctor encounter.

In the meantime, Health Telematics has added many new possibilities of changing, distorting, manipulating medical data. Most of these possibilities can be explained with reference to medical imaging as an example (e.g. in PictureArchiving and Communication System PACS).

The fields of molecular medicine and virtual reality are the latest technologies with a far reaching impact on this development.

Fig. 3: Schematic drawing to illustrate the documentation space with three dimensiones. Key parameters for the conventional documentation are shown. The box represents the conventional doctor-patient encounter with well established legal rules.

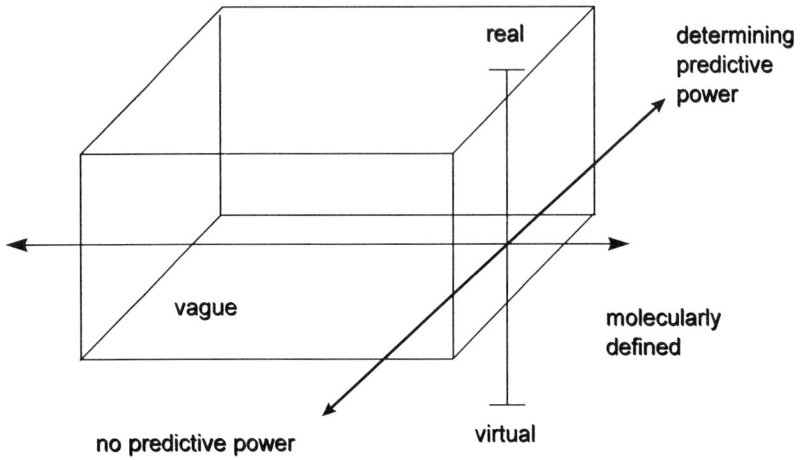

At first glance, the approach may look theoretical for those not familiar with the developments. However, it is based on international discussions which were launched by Kluge from Victoria, Canada, talking in 1989 about the „Human Analogue". A continuation of this debate has followed the discussions about the use of health data cards for storing medical records and the development of improved coding systems. In the meantime, major new data protection issues arise from molecular medicine.[70] Virtual reality applications add complicated issues. These matters are closely related to the legal issues in digital image processing, an area where it becomes increasingly complex to define the legal status of the medical document called an image. Many of these questions can also be found in the debate of how intellectual property rights can be secured.

Future workshops or EU projects regarding medical documentation and patient records needs to define in detail which segments of the n-dimensional space they adress. Failing this, discussions about legal consequences or boundaries may lead to nothing.

[70] Some of these problems became known some decades ago with Chorea Huntington Archives.

Consequences of this model for legal aspects, interface design, etc.

The model is very helpful for the understanding of why the traditional legal construct safeguarding the patient-doctor encounter cannot be the general model for all other types of medical documents. Rather, the more one moves into networking, manipulating, and compressing etc.. the more new appropriate regulations have to be identified. The key question is how much of these new problems can be solved through private law (e.g. contracts) and how much public law will be needed. This again has a major impact on interface design and the definitions of necessary security levels.

It was found that the digital signature technique, as e.g. described in the TrustHealth 1 deliverables is today the furthest developed security approach in the above mentioned conventional doctor-patient relationship. Nevertheless, the model may not be applicable in relation to some niches of the multidimensional documentation space.

Bearing this in mind, it becomes easier to understand why security issues and specifically the digital signature issue are so controversially discussed in EU Member States; frequently the points of references are insufficiently defined. Experts in this legal field tend to forget the different national legal and cultural backgrounds which are also a part of that framework. It further explains why the Ministries of Health in Europe, having failed to recognise the potential of telemedicine, are unaware of the implicit and growing legal concerns. Representatives of these ministries did not foresee the future Health Telematics world and therefore perceived little reason for any legal developments.

The discussions that took place during both SIREN workshops revealed that, throughout the European Union, health care is regulated through a great number of sometimes very diverse pieces of legislation and regulation on both national and regional level. For the moment, it is thus unrealistic to envisage any consolidation of legislation in the field of health care telematics at short term. This may be the underlying reason why many technical R & D projects shy away from the question of security. It is difficult to built complex security architectures into regional networking projects. It is further difficult to evaluate to what extent such security technology and in particular authentication systems will be in accordance with the legal framework relevant for a regional network project. For the moment the solution may be in the establishment of codes of ethics and good practice and in the conclusion of contracts between the participating parties.

In several countries with rather strong professional organisations, specifically for academically trained health professionals, the next step could be guiding regulations within professional ordinances. In the long run, this approach could also be appropriate for harmonisation on European level. However, one has to keep in mind that the structure and mission statements of various professional organisations differ in the various European Member countries. Nevertheless, collaboration and agreement between professional bodies may be important steps to clarify the legal situation.

The issue of whether in the long run there would be the need for a specific Health Telematics directive in the European Union was subject to much discussion. However, no agreement was reached on whether such a directive is a realistic project in view of the fact that health care is subject to subsidiary and falls outside the competence of the European Union.

The specifies of the legal situation in national health care systems are enormous. They directly relate to long socio-historical backgrounds and cultures, and sometimes traumatic historical events in some countries (e. g. the data protection issue is much more sensitive in countries which experienced totalitarian governments in recent history, such as Latin America or Germany). Countries with regional structures have specific regional (or in Germany "Länder") health care regulations. This has become increasingly true for the health care system of the United States. Consequently, it is still not possible in the United States to find an easy approach to telemedicine if the service is crossing the border of a state. Most experts we approached agreed that sector specific legislation will be necessary for the electronic transmission of health related data within the European Union. Such instruments can in turn deal with the diverse cultural backgrounds.

Over the last few decades, constant medical and/or technical developments ensue growing complexity in the relevant legal aspects. Subsections of this development are illustrated over a period of 30 years, starting from the time when it became clear that a new legal issue had arisen.

Fig. 4: The circles stand for an attempt to graphically represent the metamodel using the example of data protection in health care. It illustrates that technical developments are taking place which require new legal developments. As the technical development happens very quickly in current information technology it is natural that the legal situation is not adaequately adjusted. It also explains, why the common call "for legal classification" is not reflective the dynamics of the issue.

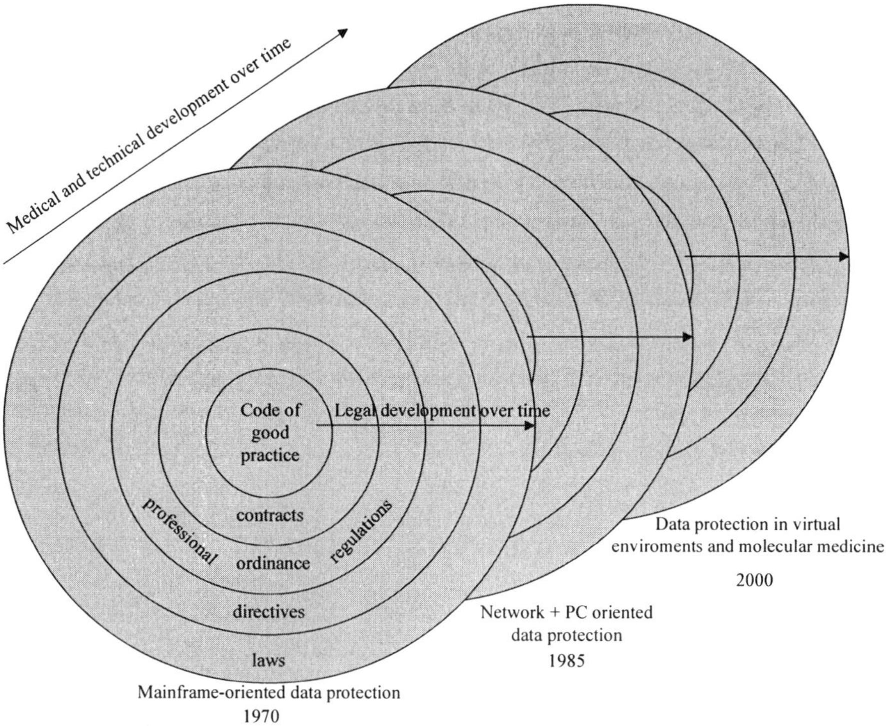

Medical and technical innovations can over a long period of time be divided into phases, each of which require new legal considerations. Usually, there is a lapse of time of several years before an effective regulation of a given legal, technical and social environment is found. The legal development may move from a flexible solution, e. g. codes and contracts, to mandatory solutions, e. g. laws and regulations. These developments rarely progress in a continuous fashion and often contain discontinuities. Thus, it is extremely difficult to be knowledgeable about the status of this process in relation to different nations, different medical, technical or legal issues. This fact explains why so few individuals are available who overlook these developments. They usually need a substantial understanding of the various dimensions of this process. Primarily technically, legally or medically oriented individuals can only focus on islands of the development.

This explains the experience of many bitter discussions between doctors and lawyers or lawyers and engineers about who has to do what to move ahead. It also explains the experience that the number of experts who formulate legal solutions in Health Telematics has been so limited in the various countries.

It takes many years to become an expert in the field and the social rewards for being such an expert in this field are limited, except for a handful of positions in academia, government and specialised consultancy firms.

The lack of a well defined legal model with fixed parameters and interrelations also explains, why legal experts at the 1st Legal Workshop battled with their task: regarding the complexity of the analytic job it had been an impossible mission.

Fixed models/concepts of medical documents or their corresponding security needs are neither theoretically nor practically meaningful. Every solution has to relate to specific definitions of the kind of documentation subject to regulation.

Thus, there will be no general health care solution, but rather security and legal solutions for specific frameworks defined through the documentation process.

5. Specific Issues in Health Care

5.1. Case Registries

Since Western medicine adapted the rules of scientific research, statistical methodology has become more and more important and held the limelight after the World War II. During the war, the first major medical documentation was established using punch cards: the registry of diseases in the German Army. When this registry was destroyed by fire in 1945, it had collected more than 7 million cases in machine-readable form.

The growing interest in case data led to more and more disease-oriented data collections which sometimes covered complete regions or countries. The development of registries was more successful in countries with state-medicine systems like in the East bloc. Data protection legislation made it difficult to build up registries; some of them even had to close down. This led many researchers to adopt a critical attitude towards strict data protection rules (see also chapter 5.3).

Some countries and states issued laws regulating the set-up and operation of medical registries. Most of these regulations refer to cancer registries. Some of those legal instruments make it quite difficult to understand the legal implications of international multi- center studies or registries. This is true for epidemiological registries, clinical studies, and clinical follow-up registries.

As there is not clear-cut the distinction between the different study types resulting, it is not easy to build up registries or to link them to operational health data from quality management initiatives. The country with the most complex legal structure in this respect is Germany, where many laws on this issue were coded on the Länder level, and many regulations are embedded in the social security laws. As described in this report, mutual regulations may help in such difficult situations. Following such an approach, the German Data-Protection Officers and the epidemiology community agreed on and widely published a common understanding of practice.

The difficult legal issue of registries may have an enormous impact on the legal acceptability of various architectures for electronic patient registers - specifically virtual or federated approaches.

So far these interferences have not been thoroughly evaluated and understood. However, in the context of the far reaching R&D programmes of the EU, such evaluation and understanding may be indispensable.

5.2. Biosignals and Images

The discussion about legal aspects of medical image systems started in the early eighties. A first assessment of the questions involved was published by Kilian in 1986. Since then, progress has been slacking. There are still many questions open - most of which deal with the definition of digital images.

The EU project EURIPACS tried to solve the problem in its legal workpackage LEGIS, which co-operated closely with the European Radiology Society. However, no convincing solution was found.

The matter is technically tackled in the most important standardisation agreement regarding digital images (DICOM), in which a new module addresses security in image communication and archiving.

An interdisciplinary workshop on how to lawfully work with digital images in health care was held in Göttingen in November 1997. The result was that for evidence reasons the workflow of currently available biosignal and image archiving and communication systems (PACS) has to be further advanced. The introduction of digital signatures is complex and needs more attention.

5.3. Medical Research

Some questions of research have already been dealt with in chapter 5.1. Here, another legal aspect shall be mentioned as it may have a major impact on how medical databases can be managed. It is the question whether the patient-secret shall be extended from the classical health professional to the computer specialist or the researcher who is working with medical data.

The discussion is referred to as “Forschungsgeheimnis“, and in relation to this term is also going on in other European countries, e.g. the Netherlands. It follows the principal idea of the early seventies, when it was discussed whether medical databases should be maintained in organisations which are headed by physicians. At that time it was the apprehension, that by such a declaration and professional link medical data would remain under the patient/ physician’s secret. It was understood that the patient/physician secret gives a much stricter guaranty for privacy than the data protection laws.

It is known that these early thoughts did not come through and that medical data is moving around through medical networks far away from the privacy castle of the direct patient-physician encounter. Thus, the old discussion has come up again with some new ideas enriched.

The main new idea is to formulate a second privacy castle which is something like an extension to the physician-patient encounter and which is the house for researchers working with medical data. This idea has the advantage that medical data is more strictly secure in the research areas. However, more researchers are easily allowed to access personal data. The two main problems in this discussion are legal ones:

1. Who is defining which person is a researcher, and how is research defined?
2. Does this extension of the strict privacy rules for the physician-patient encounter into the research area severely hinder the work of police and criminal courts?

So far, there is no consensus on the matter. The discussion in the Netherlands tends to a negative conclusion regarding the introduction of the “Forschungsgeheimnis”, while in Germany, the pros and cons are still debated. One of the pioneer organisations in the data protection field, the Data Privacy Commission of the State of Hesse, organised a workshop on this issue in 1998 which concluded a more positive statement after two days of discussions.

5.4 Medical Networks

In most European member states health care institutions of different kind organise work-flows and cooperation with so-called "medical networks". In some countries this is well structured and supported by governmental activities in others it is evolutionary or chaotic, depending of point of view. In many cases networked doctors are very enthusiastic in the beginning and very frustrated after some time. Many of them repeat for themselves the old experience that an organisational model or business model has to precede the technical one.

A major set back usually occurs, when doctors or institutions realize that some legal questions, specifically liability questions remain unanswered. A good example is the big radiological network in the State of Saxony, Germany, which nearly broke down because the liability aspect could not be clarified.

The SIREN work suggests, that in the planning of medical networks a clear step has to be executed before start: legal analysis. Similar recommendations stem from other sources, specifically the SEISMED/ISHTAR project.

How can one summarize the procedure? The easiest way is to work through the grid of legal conditions. The vertical columns contain the countries and their legal conditions and the horizontal rows the European legal issues as described in this report. The boxes in the grid then have to be worked out step by step - possibly a time consuming task. However, the liability dimensions described in 3.x may serve as a checklist. Such an approach may help to lose less medical networking projects on their way from idea to real function.

6. Outlook

A few years ago one would have expected countries to continue their legal tradition as it emerged through the course of their history. This position is still predominant when analysing the difficulties which legal systems encounter in handling the concept of the digital signature.

The national differences between the legal evolution evoked by the implementation of security technology in health care are difficult to evaluate. It will take some three or four decades of development before it can be judged how the different legal systems have been able to adapt to the information society. So far, none of the approaches has shown any advantage.

There is a substantial danger that different national legal policies (e.g. cryptography) may bring an end to cross-border Health Telematics projects e. g. the crypto-legislation in France may become a problem for the transmission of encrypted data from Germany.

Several countries have already started to adapt national legislation to the challenges of Health Telematics; the time for Europeanwide new solutions is running out.

The legal status of medical documents cannot be generally defined; it depends on many factors However, the results of the analysis of SIREN suggest the need for clearer definitions of medical documents to understand legal implications. The legal solutions have to be mapped against existing and upcoming concepts of:

- quality of medical data (validity, reliability, objectivity etc.),
- semantics and syntax of medical data,
- medical linguistics and coding of information,
- pragmatic aspects of dealing with medical data (e.g. the problem oriented record etc.), etc.

It may well mean, that such an approach helps to define interfacing concepts, including parameters defining the security of environments. However, a realistic analysis of the question and subsequent co-operation with other European and international projects need a major new activity, which may be established within the 5th Framework Programme.

National geographical conditions as well as different degrees of physician coverage has lead to very different functional models of telemedicine-services. The key issue in this context is whether services may be offered directly to a patient without an intermediary health professional who is liable to the patient.

It is to be analysed whether the quality of health can be raised for populations by means of telematics and which (traditional) existing legal regulations have to be changed to make those qualities available to the patients.

At the end of four years of work dealing with the issue of this report the authors and editors are watching new activities in many countries regarding the difficult issue.

Two major ones shall be mentioned:

1. the "Privacy of Individually Identifiable Health Information" (PIIHI) proposed rules (published 11/1999) made under HIPPA 1996 particularly in the light of the EU/USA data privacy negotiations, and
2. the coming paper of the European Commission on "Legal Aspects of Networked Health Care" to be published in 2001.

Security and liability aspects will become major components of future technology assessment projects regarding IT-use in health care.

7. Materials

7.1. GHAP Conference Recommendations (2000)

The G8 **G**lobal **H**ealth Care **A**pplications **P**roject (GHAP) has clearly proven two issues during the years since its inauguration in 1995:

- Telematics has an impressive potential for the delivery of efficient, sustainable, and accessible health care,
- international working parties for the development of applications, the harmonisation of standards, and the development of international interoperability were very successful under the G8 umbrella.

A continuation of such activities – allowing also the voluntary inclusion of non G8 countries – in limited and selected areas is strongly advised. Nearly all groups want to continue – and ask for endorsement within the G8 context.

During the final conference in Berlin from 3.5. to 5.5.2000 many recommendations and results were presented which gave a well-balanced state-of-the-art picture of the field. They are documented in the conference proceedings. Altogether they give the impression that by the use of Telematics, health care has reached a similar historical step as with the first definition of social security schemes in 1881 by Bismarck. During the conference some aspects have been considered to be so urgent or new that they were specifically addressed in the concluding sessions. They can be divided into three sections:

- new relevant content for additional research,
- urgent methodological questions, and
- organizational issues regarding the continuation of the work processes.

New relevant content for follow-up activities

1. Telematics can substantially improve the implementation of quality management in health care. This holds true for workflow improvements, introduction of evidence based medicine and general methods of quality management.
2. The rapidly growing market for international curricula in health care of all levels is demanding international work on the accreditation of such curricula and their continuous evaluation.
3. The speeding up of the harmonisation of main-stream standards is particularly promising in the context of XML.

4. Reimbursement schemes for telemedicine are necessary for the further development of this way to practice medicine.

5. Current development of card systems means that they have the potential to become internationally interoperable security tools for communication of patient data and the patient controlled data storage in virtual archives.

6. Work on nomenclatures has to continue including research on meta-directories.

7. The potential of Telematics to help victims in the case of disasters (such as earthquakes or major transport incidents) is dramatic. This options needs much more attention. Collaboration with ITU is required to open no-cost options for these relief activities.

Urgent methodological questions

1. Currently available technology assessment methodology is not usable for evaluation tasks in the dynamic IT environment. Urgent action is necessary to develop appropriate instruments.

2. Mobile phone systems in connection with smart devices, nets and intelligent home concepts offer totally new ways to organise health services, especially for the monitoring of the patient's condition at home. These options, their pros and cons have to be explored and evaluated.

3. The digital divide is becoming a major long-term problem between countries, regions in countries, and different social groups. Research is required on whether Telematics may offer ways to leapfrog the traditional development cycles. In the case of health this may lead to totally different patient centred processes.

Organisational issues regarding the continuation of the work processes

1. Participants wished to continue the work under the endorsement of G8 countries and the G8 logo.

2. An informal infrastructure is necessary for the organisation of working team meetings. This infrastructure could be established immediately through a collaboration of existing regional groups like EHTEL in Europe and MEDIS in Japan.

3. Working meetings have to be arranged between the different working groups in regular discussions following the course of their work.

4. Results shall be presented in connection to major international Telematics conferences, e.g. MEDINFOs (next in 2001 in London) or regional IMIA conferences in Asia, the America, or Africa.

5. Within the next three years it should be explored whether WHO or ITU or other existing international agencies can take over the G8 working groups into a new mainline activity of improving the world's health by the use of evaluated Telematic systems.

It was generally agreed that progress will remain slow if the professionals in the health care systems are not becoming better informed and able to take advantage of the options which Telematics is offering to them. The same holds true for the degree of investment into IT in health care, which is surprisingly low in relation to all other sectors of the national economies.

It was decided at the end of the conference that an invitation by Russia, being the new G8 member, to host the follow-up working conference of the G8 GHAP activities in St. Petersburg or Moscow in 2001 would be welcomed.

Berlin, 6 May 2000
Otto Rienhoff
Chair, Concluding Session

Note:
The Publication "Health Care in the Information Age - National and International Challenges from the G8 Global Healthcare Applications Project (GHAP); Vol. 2 Recommendations and Results of the GHAP Final Conference" by Dietzel, G., Dietel, M., Nerlich, M., Rienhoff, O., Ricke, J., and Ammann, A. (eds.) will be available in 2000 from IOS Press, Amsterdam.

7.2. The Einbeck Recommendations on Legal Aspects of Telemedicine (1999)

1. Telemedicine facilitates and supports medical services independently of geographical barriers by combining telecommunications and informatics (telematics). The possible applications of telemedicine have grown over the past few years as regards both their quality and quantity. But this does not imply the birth of a new medical discipline. Rather, it means a growing potential to improve both the quality and efficiency of medical services. For instance, expert knowledge can be made available to a patient at any time and in any place.
2. Since it is independent of both the temporal and geographical barriers that usually prevent contact between patients and carers, telemedical services are predestined for cross-sector applications. Telemedicine can thus contribute to solving problems that arise from the separation of ambulatory and hospital care.
3. The possible applications of telemedicine are primarily distinguished by their effects upon the doctor-patient relationship, such as:

   (a) the use of telemedicine in the "background" to a treatment, for instance in the continuous education of health professionals, for external archiving or for anonymous second opinions. Here telemedicine is used in a supplementary function;
   (b) the use of telemedicine to co-operate with a specialist either as a consulting physician or in the direct treatment of a patient; and
   (c) the formation of a self-sufficient, direct relationship between the doctor and the patient, as takes place with so-called "cyber docs".

4. Using telemedicine, however, gives rise to specific legal questions in areas where differing standards mean that it is not possible to adopt a common approach to the use of telemedicine in all health care sectors. The following recommendations sum up the legal problems that need to be solved as well as the legal challenges that arise from using telemedicine.
5. Telemedicine requires co-operation in fields that have so far been dominated by individual consultations. It brings about new choices for the patient by encouraging links and networks between health professionals across many disciplines, rather than the division of health care into individual, specialised sectors. Due to the considerable increase in the flow of information as well as the improved availability of expert knowledge, telemedicine may enable patients to better understand issues relating to their health and treatment, thus supplying them with more efficient

decision support for making informed choices about their care. The patient may hence be enabled to take on more responsibility in the treatment process which will in turn ensure a more successful outcome to that treatment.

6. In this way, telemedicine helps support the patient on their way to becoming an emancipated and independent participant in the health care system. However, telemedicine should not become an end in itself, but lead to improvements in the quality of health care. It should promote a holistic approach to the patient thus strengthening the development of a trusting relationship between doctors and patients as partners.

7. The principle of personal consultations has to be modified with regard to telemedicine, however. Telemedicine should only replace a "face-to-face" consultation between the patient and their carer if it can be guaranteed that there will be no significant shortcomings in the quality and standard of care provided to them.

8. The principles which have been developed in the jurisprudence and laid down in professional laws concerning the treatments that it is illegal to give by "remote-control" also apply to telemedicine. For example, telesurgical operations directed by a doctor who is unable, if necessary, to personally intervene in the procedure, are not permitted.

9. To take full advantage of telemedicine's inherent possibilities for improving the quality and efficiency of care, technical errors and communication gaps between the different media involved must be avoided by the ubiquitous use of homogenous exchange formats, which itself will require a high degree of harmonisation of communication standards.

10. National health care institutions and insurance companies cannot act alone in making decisions where the development, application and extension of telemedicine is at stake: insurers, health professionals and insurants have to agree upon the extent of innovation and how it will be funded. For this purpose it will also be indispensable to integrate an adequate rating of telemedical services into existing tariffs. Any further development of revenue systems must also take into account the potential for cross-border consultations, especially within the Member States of the European Union, where the patients' right to claim medical services beyond national borders will necessitate the introduction of cross-border cost reimbursement systems.

11. The same standard of care provided by a specialist in a face-to-face consultation with a patient must also be guaranteed for a patient who is treated via a telemedical application. Simply because telemedicine allows the more efficient integration of expert knowledge in a way that could enable it to exceed the level of knowledge of an individual specialist does not neccesarily mean that the standard of care will be improved.

12. The principle of the doctor's free choice of methods of treatment remains unchanged by telelemedicine, that is, they are still free to choose the method they prefer according to their training, experience and practice. That means that telemedical applications will only become ubiquitous when:

(a) their beneficial effects are, on the whole, incontestable;
(b) they are generally available in more than just a few special centres; and
(c) in a given case - and in comparison to traditional treatment methods - they bear less risk, less stress factors for the patient or promise better therapeutic outcomes.

13. The patient must be informed of any special risks associated with a particular telemedicine application.
14. As long as telemedicine is not generally established as a treatment standard, a physician in whose practice or clinic this technology is not available is not obliged to draw his patients' attention to other institutions offering such possibilities, i.e., such situations do not yet fall under the physician's legal duty of extended patient information with reference to alternative treatment methods.
15. The various possibilities that telemedicine brings about for the creation, storage, transmission, sharing and alteration of electronic medical information does not alter the physician's responsibilities regarding such information. Furthermore, it must be possible to verify the origin, quality and integrity of transferrred medical data.
16. Legally speaking, the professional colleague who is consulted by a doctor who started a treatment ("Primärbehandler) remains a consulting physician ("Konsiliararzt") in telemedical applications just as he does in conventional practice, unless he takes over the direction of the treatment process, thus changing status and becoming a co-doctor ("Mitbehandler"). In the majority of the cases, the consulting physician is the patient's contract partner and therefore liable as far as is laid down in the respective contract. This is so where inpatient treatment is given on the basis of a split hospital contract ("gespaltener Krankenhausvertrag"), a staff doctor contract or a contract for a practitioner with hospital affiliation ("Belegarztvertrag"), as well as in the case of ambulatory care. If the patient is treated on the basis of a full hospital admission contract ("totaler Krankenhausaufnahmevertrag") the consulting physician legally acts on behalf of the hospital employer. The consulting physician has to answer for damage brought about through his own fault according to general liability principles. Even when executing an order, the consulting physician still bears his own examination duties ("Prüfungspflichten").

If he overlooks the obvious errors of his colleague who started the treatment, he is liable because of insufficient control of plausibility. In the case of errors which occur due to a breakdown in communication or organization during the telemedical application, the primary principles of organizational responsibility ("Organisations-verschulden") will apply.

17. To avoid conflicts between national legal standards in the area of medical liability, both doctor and patient should agree on a choice of law and stipulate a jurisdiction ("Rechtswahl und Gerichtsstandvereinbarung") that will apply to cross-border telemedical applications. International efforts to evolve cross-border regulations for telemedical liability questions urgently need support.

18. Existing data protection laws are inadequate since they do not take into account any of the specific uses of information and communication technologies in telemedical practice. Nor may the amendment of data protection laws that is required by the European Union's Directive on data protection offer sufficient answers to crucial issues regarding security and privacy in telemedicine applications. Verification is therefore required regarding whether or not only new and specific legislation for health-related data will be able to bridge the data protection gap or whether it would be sufficient to amend existing data protection laws. In each case, specific factors relating to medical practice and research, as well as to the use of data collected from these areas should be more adequately provided for than in the existing general data protection laws. This would lead to more legal certainty which, in turn, could boost the further development of patient-oriented telemedicine.

19. The transfer and exchange of medical information in telemedical applications must always be legitimated by the patient's consent. That means that the patient must be informed about the nature of the telemedical application, its risks and any alternative means of transferring their data. The consent must be in writing and laid down in an appropriate document. When transferring patient data to non-European Union countries, special precautions for security have to be taken or the patient must give their specific consent.

To achieve maximum data security the amount of data transferred in telemedical applications should be reduced to the absolute minimum (minimum principle, anonymity, pseudonymity). Furthermore, the interests of data security require the use of generally accepted safety devices, namely the most recent techniques for encoding and digital signature. However, even with these devices, the absolute protection of data cannot be guaranteed, especially as advances in cryptography that will allow the decoding of data that seem to be well protected today are not out of the question in the future.

These aspects do not prevent the use of telemedicine but careful consideration must always be given to its risks and advantages. This may sometimes lead to some necessary restrictions being placed upon its use.

Deutsche Gesellschaft für Medizinrecht e.V. (DGMR)
(German Society for Health Care Law)
Einbeck, 31st October 1999

Note:
The Publication "Rechtsfragen der Telemedizin" by Dierks, C., Feussner, H., and Wienke, A. (eds.) will be available in 2000 from Springer Verlag, Heidelberg.

7.3. SIREN Workshops 1998/1996

7.3.1. The 2nd Legal Workshop of SIREN (1998)

Since the first workshop at the end of 1996 the legal and security issues in networking had raised increasing interest (see chapter II B 2 for development of e.g. digital signature regulations). It was, therefore, considered necessary to collect further information on the specific impact of this general development on the health sector. In addition, it was thought important to list the security policies for health care networking adopted by the national Ministries of Health, as well as their approaches to the issue of regulating the information society in health care.

Recruitment of Experts for the Second SIREN Legal Workshop

Following the recommendations of the project reviewers, the Second Legal Workshop comprised three groups of people:

1. Representatives of Telecom providers (large companies) preparing TTP and security services for the European market.
2. Representatives of national ministries of health or social affairs dealing with the questions of secure communication within their health care system.
3. High ranking experts in the field of combined knowledge about legal aspects, medical aspects and information technology aspects.

Following some initial discussions, the planning of the workshop was agreed in a first draft paper. Several senior legal people acted as chairperson or rapporteur. Some fifty people/organisations were contacted, but due to their limited availability the workshop went ahead with some twenty participants. However, many of those unable to attend the workshop in Frankfurt wished to remain on the mailing list and to participate in the validation phase of the activity. Hence, it was decided to draw up a validation matrix for those involved in the legal work-package of SIREN or for contenders who had declared a interest in future collaboration.

Legal Experts

Professor Kuner and Professor Burkhardt of the Legal Advisory Board of the European Commission were approached, but were both unable to come. Professor Roßbach, who undertook the first empirical research in Germany on how to replace paper documents in courts, and Professor Kilian from Hannover are two other leading experts who were highly interested, but not available for the Frankfurt meeting. Similarly well-known names in other European countries were also approached. During this recruiting phase, the SIREN group to notice, that most of these leading experts had no senior deputies who could participate in the project. It appears that a general lack of funding makes it impossible for research institutions to employ senior deputy academics. Hence, such institutions are headed by senior, experienced and very busy academics who lead a group of junior researchers.

It is probable that no more than 60 and 100 such experts can be found in the European Union.

Representatives from Health Ministries

From work previously undertaken within the G 7 Projects, it had transpired that only two health ministries (namely France and Sweden) are active in health care network security, promoting experts in this field. Whilst several other countries currently define their needs as to legislation regarding telematics in health care including security aspects, most European ministries of health lack relevant structures or working groups working on these issues. There is a general belief that digital signatures policies are the responsibility of other ministries, such as the Ministry of Justice or Ministry of Interior. In some countries, civil servant lawyers concerned with the regulation of health care systems were actually unaware of the fact that digital signatures or cryptography issues may be relevant to their mission. Noticeable was a North-South divide, which showed most Northern European countries taking an interest in the matter, whilst in the South this can only be said of Italy and Spain.

Noteworthy is the fact that our persistent request for experts from the health care ministries seems to have created a demand for more information.

Industry - Major Companies

The assumption that the major telecom operators are moving into a new market of security services and trusted third party services for health care is misplaced. Several of the major companies, such as German Telecom were not inclined to provide an expert. It appears that following a long period of market investment, previoulsy optimistic expectations to exploit such services were lowered due to complex market regulation. The same can be said about providers of Hospital Information Systems.

Hence, a major European computer service provider had to admit that, following the creation of a security division lead by a former high-ranking privacy commissioner and despite much advertising, many exhibitions and projects, not a single contract to set up a trusted third party service had as yet been signed.

Similar ambitions to develop electronic commerce in Europe have also been dashed (contrary to the US).

In a great many companies technical security experts were among the staff while experts with a legal backround were conspicuously absent. Hence, the few workshop participants from industry tended to have technical training.

The SIREN Legal Workshop

On Thursday 3rd and Friday 4th September 1998 a Workshop was hosted at the Kassenärztliche Vereinigung Hessen in Frankfurt am Main, Germany, by the Physician's Chamber of Lower Saxony (PCSL), formally responsible for Workpackage 4 of the SIREN project. The Workshop was entitled "Legal Aspects of Security in Health Networks". The aims of the Workshop were:

- To give an overview of national legal approaches
- To describe the legal issues regarding electronic health care documents
- To understand the legal impact of digital signatures in health care
- To create a priority list for national actions towards a legal framework
- To prepare a European list of actions

Overview of National Legal Approaches

The legal situation regarding the use of digital signatures and electronic documents in health care in the fifteen Member States of the European Union was researched and analysed (see chapter136 ff). Prior to the Workshop, background papers were circulated to the delegates, including an overview of national and European laws, together with an *ad hoc* questionnaire to collect up-to-date information on the legal situation in the participating countries.

Legal Issues Regarding Electronic Health Care Documents and Digital Signatures

The delegates at the Workshop, representing a broad cross-section of expertise and outlook in medical informatics and Health Telematics, were able to review and identify the key legal questions and challenges surrounding the transition from paper-based to electronic documentation in medicine and health care that must be understood and resolved before that transition can take place.

Electronic documents

The delegates raised a number of concerns regarding electronic documents:

- At a European level, a proper legal definition of an "electronic document", describing its validity and efficacy does not exist but is badly needed.
- European law should create a framework in which electronic documents can be freely used. The need to modernise the legal regime throughout Europe in order to prepare for the "hospital without walls" is a question of necessity and not possibility.
- The vendors of health informatics technology and the users of this technology need to know the legal consequences of using electronic documents and digital signatures - both at present and in the future.
- We also need to know the legal consequences of the transition from paper to electronic documents and vice versa (printing an electronic document onto paper for example).
- As respects ownership we need to know who legally owns the data or, indeed, if it can be owned at all. Does the patient own it? What are the access rights for practitioners and patients to medical records?
- Regarding the appropriate level of regulations for electronic documents: what is the most appropriate level at which legislation should be created in order to best facilitate the international exchange of electronic health care documents, the development of pan-European medical services and the free movement of medical expertise?

Digital signatures

Regarding digital signatures, it was felt that further clarification was required through national and/or European Union legislators regarding several matters.

- The existence of digital signatures - for what purposes in electronic communication in health care must or should digital signatures be used?
- Is it possible, allowed or even required to use digital signatures? When can they be used? Does it depend upon the sensitivity of the information contained in the document?
- In which countries do laws on digital signatures need to be implemented?
- Where are digital signatures accepted in the courts and treated as having the same evidential value as a hand-written signature?

- Should certification authorities have specific policies on digital signatures used in health care applications or will general policies be enough?
- Can digital signatures be used by natural persons, by legal persons or by both?
- Should legislation on the national level and/or European level regulate digital signatures? Should it be permissible for natural persons and/or legal persons, to use more than one digital signature in electronic health care documents?

Encryption

Regarding encryption the Workshop delegates felt that further clarification was required regarding:

- What documents have to be encrypted and on what level? Should we differentiate between email, data exchange and the archiving of medical data? Is encryption necessary in all these circumstances?
- What levels of encryption are allowed? What levels are possible?
- What other technical and organisational problems exist with regards to encryption?

Promoting professional accountability

There are specific instances - if we are to share electronic documents using digital signatures - where we need medical professionals to be entitled to use and share medical documents across the borders of Member States of the European Union.

- In the European Union's Data Protection Directive there are specific provisions relating to health records so do we, therefore, need to introduce similar health care specific provisions into a general European Union Directive or national law?
- Can we, in so doing, create a Register of health professionals maintained by a Registrar in each country in order to avoid fraud? It was agreed by all the Workshop delegates that in an environment where electronic documents are ubiquitous we will need a system whereby we can verify a doctor's qualifications and be sure of their proper registration and right to practice for instance, when sending medical records such as x-rays or ultrasound scans, or when receiving an electronic prescription to be prepared for a patient.
- There are many different types of documents in medicine and therefore many different types of signature - e.g., automatic results from machines, signed laboratory reports, doctor's opinions and so forth. A key problem in a harmonised European environment will be the clear imposition of liability for the authenticity and accuracy of a document. For instance, if it is acceptable for a nurse in the

United Kingdom to sign a laboratory report but not acceptable in France for anyone other than a doctor to do so, how can a nurse-signed document from the UK be accepted in France? Moreover, even if an institution does have procedures in place to protect documents it may still have to answer issues of liability in court, though digital signatures are a way of demonstrating we have used the state-of-the-art to try and protect confidentiality so they are important for the risk management of health care institutions using electronic documents. If electronic documents have different uses to paper documents then naturally different regulations should apply to them. In health care there is a greater need to balance security against the need for speedy access to medical records in an emergency whereas in banking and commerce it easier to make security a high priority more of the time. Because of the de-centralisation of health care in many areas, e.g., with a move towards more nurse practitioners, the type as well as the frequency of emergency medical situations is changing. Will digital signatures need to be a mandatory form of security protection for cross-border transmissions?

Legal Impact of Digital Signatures in Health Care

How and why will digital signatures and related concepts change the way in which health care professionals communicate with each other and the way in which health care itself is delivered to patients? The Workshop delegates examined the changes that digital signatures will inevitably bring to the regulatory framework surrounding the creation, storage and transmission of health care records.

The doctor-patient relationship

A patient is a different kind of consumer to the person purchasing electrical goods or even to a client in a bank. The patient's relationship with the health care professional is of a fiduciary nature and it has the specific characteristic of being rooted in the question of human existence. Furthermore, a patient is usually physically and psychologically in a vulnerable position and health care is still based on a paternalistic element.

To the extent that the patient / health care professional relationship is of a specific nature, participants of the Workshop agreed that national legislators must consider the use of electronic documents and digital signatures in the health care sector as presenting its own unique problems which need to be individually taken into account.

Secure identification of the health care professional

A second health care specific issue that was discussed is the question of who can be considered a health care professional and who can electronically sign health care documents. It was generally felt that this issue should be addressed by national legislators. Participants believed that realistically speaking this matter will probably be regulated on a national level, but for long-term benefit there should be some European Union harmonisation, so as to enable barrier-free health care throughout Europe.

Control over the dissemination and use of health care data

A significant absence from this Workshop were representatives of professional medics and particularly representatives of patients who would be able to discuss their individual rights and duties in the context of the ownership and security of health care information and how digital signatures would impact upon these rights and duties.

A commission in the United States investigating data protection issues identified a company that was collecting individual data on people that had a higher than average likelihood of developing Alzheimer disease. They sold this database to companies that wanted to sell these "patient customers" something. This is a good example of how we can start to lose control of what people know about us and how they use that information. The patient has the right to know and consent to how their records will be manipulated - this is part of the doctor's professional and ethical duty towards their patient. In occupational health there are special issues of access by an employer to a patient's records.

In the networks of the next century insurance companies, employers and others will be a part of this network. There is the possibility of the inadvertent revelation of confidential information to someone who shouldn't have received it with grave consequences for the patient. We need to make sure that, in such instances we work on a need to know basis only and the use of digital signature hierarchies presents us with the opportunity to do this.

A Priority List for National Actions towards a Legal Framework

The Workshop delegates, through small regionally focused discussion groups, mapped out key actions and strategies that need to be implemented on a national level to allow for the full legal acceptance of digital signatures and electronic documents in the health care systems of their countries.

Though the discussions that took place in open plenary session at the Workshop can only represent the immediate views of those who attended, the national experts there present were able to identify a number of problems, remarkable by their commonality to all of their legal systems, as well as some discrete issues of concern only in specific jurisdictions.

The Workshop uncovered an urgent requirement for further collaborative research on a number of the topics that were discussed, including uses of digital signatures, to establish exactly what national laws and European guidance is needed in the health care sector.

The Workshop delegates were able to conclude priority lists for actions at a national level to address the regulation and use of digital signatures and electronic documents in the health care systems of their individual countries.

United Kingdom

- A Secure Electronic Commerce Bill would be the first step down the road but it is unclear as yet whether or not the United Kingdom needs a health care specific piece of legislation. A recognition in the law that the health care sector has special needs might suffice and this has been suggested to the Secretary of State for Health as well as to other relevant persons in the United Kingdom.
- Dependencies were not adequately discussed at the Workshop. We all have dependencies upon technology when recording a case note on paper because that case note can be lost. If an entire system, hosting a large number of health records, is lost then the damage can be very extensive. It should therefore be a legal requirement to have extensive backup and archiving procedures. This should become a legal requirement rather than simply a best practice procedure (though not following this would, of course, be a breach of the duty of care principle). We need a back up regime that is good enough for us to trust.
- We need to balance the need to create audit trails with the rights of the patient to rectify their records if they contain inaccuracies. The data protection rules need to fit comfortably with the audit trial rules - they do not at the moment. There is a definition of “health care professional” in the UK’s Data Protection Act 1998 - this could be cross-referenced with another piece of domestic legislation.
- There is a danger of different standards arising in allied professions. Doctors are still legally required to keep paper records but these are easily lost. The health care system in the UK is already awash with delegated legislation - we really do not need lots and lots more.
- In the United Kingdom we cannot currently envisage the creation of new health care specific legislation on encryption or digital signatures - though general legislation will come in the next session of Parliament. There appears little that is truly specific to health care with the possible exception of professional hierarchies, that is, who is allowed to receive what, and how. If the Government intends ordinary people to have digital signatures, though, this position may change - it becomes an ID of sorts and inherent proof that the patient is who he or she really says they are. In this case, individuals should only be allowed one digital signature in the health domain - otherwise you could go and get three prescriptions under three different names. Though in other countries this is not the case - the use of any

name other than that which appears on your birth certificate - your given name - is prohibited. One solution could be use of biometric identifiers as a backup check: defining digital signatures differently and more strictly than in general, though this brings with it significant ethical problems.

- There will also need to be harmonisation of the laws governing when an electronic contract is concluded - in the United Kingdom a cash withdrawal from an Automatic Teller Machine (ATM) is a binding contract - not so in the rest of Europe. Interfaces will be required between national certification authorities and this would be an appropriate area in which the Directive could make provision.
- There is a very urgent need for a registration system that prevents the forgery of training certificates and bogus doctors. Could a digital signature become, effectively, a form of national ID card by the back door?

Sweden and Denmark

- Authenticity is a central concept underlying criminal, procedural, administrative, evidential and civil legal questions. A document must give the reader reason to believe that the text originates from the individual who, according to the record, is seen to be the originator.
- Clarification is required of what is a "patient record" and what is "other material" in an electronic health care system. We need to know where the borderlines exist, whether the law recognises electronic forms, whether it has to be signed (and if so if digital signatures are allowed) and what documents fall outside of these signature requirements.
- The role of consent and veracity - in the health care sector we need consent from patients, recorded in some way and fixed in the electronic document so it is known. Veracity is a concept within documents and will not create special problems in the electronic environment if the law is not strict.
- Long time storage and issues of migration need to be dealt with.

Germany

- Changes need to be made in the civil code in order to give equivalence between hand-written documents and electronic documents.
- An analysis of what specific regulations in the health care sector are necessary should be undertaken. We need to establish clearly whether it is strictly necessary to have a separate TTP structure and system for the health care sector or if we can use the existing structure.

- There is a need to clarify the ownership of patient records and patient rights.

Greece

- Greece faces a similar situation to Germany so all of the national action points proposed for Germany are also relevant to the legal situation in Greece.
- Changes need to be made in the civil code in order to give equivalence between hand-written documents and electronic documents.
- An analysis of what specific regulations in the health care sector are necessary should be undertaken. We need to establish clearly whether it is strictly necessary to have a separate TTP structure and system for the health care sector or if we can use the existing structure.
- There is a need to clarify the ownership of patient records and patient rights.
- Moreover, electronic documents should be recognised as admissible evidence and receive a similar status to paper documents, provided that an equivalent mechanism to the hand-written signature will be established.
- Accordingly, it will be necessary to change the current social security legislation which is based upon paper documents.

Belgium and the Netherlands

- As a general remark, the Belgian and Dutch delegations stressed that, in their view, both the Belgian and the Dutch Ministries of Health need to become more aware of current information technology developments in health care, such as the possibilities of using digital signatures. This need for awareness also exists within medical insurance companies. An action programme by these Ministries of Health, like the Dutch Government's (1994) Action Programme for the Information Superhighway71 would be very much appreciated. The key word on respect of the medical data is trust. We can reach this trust by providing good regulations (if necessary legislation) for electronic health care documents. Important subjects are the confidentiality, integrity, availability and authenticity of medical data. In the end, this should lead to better medical treatment within the European Union. This is to be achieved by means of, e.g., encryption, Certification Authorities, digital signatures and so forth to protect medical data or electronic medical documents which are in some respects already covered by the existing legal framework: the Civil Code, the Data Protection Act, etc. This existing legal framework already functions within the Belgian and Dutch health care systems.

---

71 From metaphor 'to action': http://info.minez.nl/docs/nap-en.htm.

- Electronic documents - as far as the Netherlands is concerned there is a change of law with regard to medication prescriptions and we need to screen all national legislation for similar problems. The Ministry of Justice has prepared reports on encryption for the transport and storage of medical data. We have a legal problem because there is no law on encryption - harmonisation is necessary. The registration of certification authorities for the health care sector is required and we need some kind of co-ordination - perhaps through a Chamber of Trusted Third Parties. We assume that several regulations (though not legislation) exist with regard to electronic medical documents or electronic documents in general, examples would be those rules adopted by professional organisations such as the Dutch Computer Society's (NGI) Code for Information Security by the Dutch Computer Society. An example of a Dutch law that needs to be adapted is the law that regulates medical prescriptions. This regulation requires a hand-written signature and is already considered out-of-date. In addition, it seems useful to us, to also screen other regulations (including legislation) for similarly outdated provisions.
- Digital signatures - Belgium now has a bill on digital signatures. A bill to adapt the Civil Code is now being discussed in the Belgian Parliament. Concerning health care, the Belgian SIS card is of importance. The Ministry of Social Security is now aiming to ensure they are compatible with the Bill on digital signatures. The Dutch government is more reserved in drafting legislation for digital signatures. It is not clear yet whether the Netherlands will create a digital signature law. Self-regulation has also been considered as an instrument for creating rules for digital signatures. The Netherlands will probably follow the UNCITRAL Model Law on Electronic Commerce, which contains rules for digital signatures but is likely to implement the EU Directive on digital signatures, once it has been adopted. The Dutch government has recently paid attention to the issue of digital signatures in several reports: the government report on legislation for the information highway (Ministry of Justice, February 1998), the report on Trusted Third Parties (Ministry of Economic Affairs and the Ministry of Transport, Public Works and Water Management, March 1998), and the report on electronic legal transactions (Ministry of Justice, April 1998). It is to be expected that rules for digital signatures will be set out in general regulations, not in specific health regulations.
- Encryption - the Belgium and Dutch delegations considered it important that the transport and storage of medical data is technically reliable within Europe. From a legal perspective, harmonisation of legislation will meet serious problems. It is, however, necessary to approve the transport of confidential medical data across borders. Because medical data contains very sensitive personal information, a high

level of encryption should be applied. No European Union member State should forbid using such types of encryption.

- Registers of health care professionals - in Belgium there is no law that prescribes the registration of health care professionals. Only the Belgian organisation for health care professionals has a register. In the Netherlands, the Medical Professions in Individual health care Act (*Wet BIG*) prescribes the registration of health care professionals:

  doctors, dentists, pharmacists, psychotherapists, psychologists, physiotherapists, midwives and nurses. The registration of health care professionals can be of importance with regard to the digital signature.

France

- In France the situation for digital signatures, electronic documents and encryption is not a problem and, in any event, it would be difficult to get any more laws through as Parliament is overloaded.
- France is presently preparing for the urgent problem of defining rules for sharing information that is not totally anonymous for evaluation purposes and to increase the care of the patient. This would break the secret professional laws so a new law needs to be created to make an exception - this is in preparation and is directly due to the availability of electronic medical information. The political decision to enact a new law on this subject is to be taken in the next months. For the other questions, the French philosophy is to "wait and see" how the actual legislation is adapted to the new environment created by electronic documents and networking.
- Therefore, priorities for France should be to ensure that secure electronic document creation and exchange is technically possible, simply available for users, at a low cost and with user-friendly tools. The French, in common with many of the Workshop delegates, strongly believe that if technology gets in the way of health professionals doing their jobs they simply won't use it - clinicians themselves state this time and time again.

A European List of Actions (recommended by the participants of the workshop)

Notwithstanding that health is not expressly stated to be within the European Union's competency by the Treaty of Rome, because the development of national legislation and its harmonisation on a European level could be greatly assisted by Brussels a list of priority actions was prepared for the European Commission.

Preparing for digital signatures in European health care

Neither the UNCITRAL model legislation nor the EU Directive make specific or detailed provision for the use of electronic documents and digital signatures in health care. However, the the EU Directive on Electronic Signatures does fulfil the main requirements for the utilisation of this technology in the health care sector. However, some of the peculiarities of this field will have to be taken into account if we are to facilitate the spread of digital signatures to allow for the authentication of health care professionals sending medical data and integrity control of the data transmitted on electronic networks.

Therefore, the legal modifications needed paradoxically have to be more concerned with medical law than with information technology law because the use of digital signatures forces us to examine the way we deal with medical information:

a) Harmonisation of registration evidence

Legal evidence that the people involved in a health care network are duly registered in their country as health care professionals. This implies the setting up of electronic registers in the different countries of the European Union and the development of common electronic certification controlled by national authorities.

b) Harmonisation of the protection level

The protection level which has to be implemented according to the type of documents transmitted or consulted. Some documents may require a very high security level but some others may only require a much lower level of protection. As a consequence, this will lead to harmonisation of the hierarchy of the rights of access (to read or to write the data) according to the status of the health care professional: medical practitioner, nurse, administrator and so forth. This implies the definition of a common mapping of authorisation. Common procedures (with acceptance of standards) via self-regulation on a European level should be envisaged.

c) Harmonisation of the rules for emergency access

This should enable access to the medical records in an emergency with or without a patients' consent. The security of the medical data must not decrease the security of the patient. There is a balance to establish between privacy protection and health protection. A patient must not be harmed or lose their chances of survival simply because a medical practitioner has not been able to have access to some key medical information registered in the record of the patient. In an emergency situation a procedure must be defined and controlled by a medical authority which has the ability to decide if there is a real need for emergency access to the medical record and to allow this access.

d) Definition of new rules for archiving the health care records

These rules must take into account the peculiarities of information technology and must not be based on a kind of transcription of the rules for paper archives. We must think differently and integrate into the new concept of electronic archives the security advantages provided by new technology.

e) Encryption and confidentiality

The legislation concerning the encryption of data is very diverse or even absent in the countries of the European Union, although an important harmonisation effort is actually being conducted at the national level. It has been stated that the harmonisation of this legislation appears to be a general problem with no medical specificities.

f) Certification Authorities

To reach a uniform policy at the European level, preference should be given to a European Certification Authority (like, for example, the EU Working Party on the Protection of Individuals with regard to the Processing of Personal Data, as specified in Article 29 of the EU Directive on Data Protection). It is preferable that each European Union member State should have a certification authority specifically for the health care sector. Each European Union member State should also have an institution for establishing national uniform policies for certification authorities in different sectors. One example of an existing sectoral certification authority is the Belgian Social Crossroads Bank, that carries out quality control by certifying keys for the SIS card.

g) Pseudonyms

Regarding the use of pseudonyms it was noted that patients and health care professionals can have different identities and thus can also have different digital signatures e. g. in the UK, whereas this is forbidden e. g. in Germany. With regards to the health care sector a balance must be found between accessability and the right to privacy. Concerning the patient using transborder telemedicine services this is an actual problem and may also become a problem for health professionals.

h) Security measures for the receiver

With regard to security measures for the receivers of electronic messages, it should be required that the receiver takes the necessary measures to keep medical data secure, so that when medical data has been exchanged between sender and receiver, the receiver also has obligations, evidenced by the issuing of an electronic receipt.

i) Key revocation

The Workshop highlighted an important new issue with regards to key management and the reliable timing of keys. We need to know how a key might be revoked, especially if something had already been received by someone who was expected to act upon it.

Conclusions

I. The use of digital signatures involves new types of liability - it will not be purely contractual or defined in relation to the monetary value of the transaction but will be based upon the health professional's duty of care and the related amount of possible damages.

II. We need a clearer definition of the "electronic medical record" so that we clearly know when a document we are dealing with comes under any new health care specific laws on digital signatures and electronic documents, and when reference to the existing law is sufficient. The law tends, anyway, to be sectorally specific - evidential value, the laws of contract, penal provisions and so forth are all separate branches, but new structures and new branches may be required to cope with new technology. We must learn to think differently and must not try to mould digital signatures, electronic documents and information technology in general into established definitions and concepts in order to avoid the process of change.

III. In an electronic doctor/patient transaction the doctor must know what type of transaction he is involved in and therefore what level of security applies to different types of documents. There must be (1) the mutual recognition of health care professionals, (2) liability for the authenticity, (3) accuracy of contents that is discharged by the use of certain procedures, and (4) some proof of receipt.

IV. It should be possible to use health care specific trusted third parties (TTPs) and certification authorities (CAs) which give out digitally signed certificates which denote not only the author but also his or her qualifications. We should create harmonised security standards or certificates that are health care specific, controlled by a national authority.

V. The creation of audit trials - emails sent, received and read - or other such trails which provide more evidential certainty for health care providers and also improve the quality of patient care will be essential. Time stamping who has written what and when will also be important.

VI. Regulations should be made at the European level which must be implemented by Member States through delegated legislation. The OECD released its *Recommendation of the Council concerning Guidelines for Cryptography* Policy on 27 March 1997. It would be useful to consider in what way these Guidelines can be applied to health care.

VII. The EU Directive also provides a general legal framework but national States will need to act to create stricter laws if the European Union does not intervene with a health care specific digital signature Directive or to incorporate health care definitions and concepts into the present Directive. There is already a clear danger that if no action is taken by the European Union within the next 1½ years we will probably see divergent national solutions emerging which it will take us a significant amount of time to re-harmonise and will present us with avoidable barriers to the widespread use of electronic documents across European borders.

VIII. It was recommended by the Workshop that the use of electronic documents and digital signatures across borders requires an international co-operation between national registers. We need to reach agreement about definitions of different classes of professionals, doctors, nurses, midwives and other health professionals, to allow controlled access also from out of the country in certain situations. The diverse national medical professional organisations should be encouraged to envisage the use of secure Health Telematics by acting as CA or contracting a CA.

IX. With regards to encryption, no legislation appears to be specific to the field but we do need to define a common health data communication policy in order to use digital signatures across borders.

X. We should actively contribute to the harmonisation of the management of health care data in Europe by defining a common health care data communication policy whose security will be guaranteed by the adequate use of digital signatures. This approach appeared to the Workshop delegates to be a better solution than the restriction of the possibilities provided by the EU Directive on Digital Signatures in the field of health care in order to confine its utilisation to the actual organisation based on paper communication or on some informal relations where the reaction times are short.

XI. Greater awareness needs to be created among European Health Ministries regarding the use of electronic documents and digital signatures in health care and greater support of cross-border projects should be made available. Action plans to create greater awareness among practitioners and patients should be set in motion and the views of doctors solicited through links to existing scientific and health care organisations.

7.3.2. The 1st Legal Workshop of SIREN (1996)

The first main step taken in relation to the work developed in the legal work package of the EU-project SIREN was to organise a workshop and submit the following points for discussion to legal experts of three EU Member states, namely Belgium, Germany and Sweden:

1. the need to define elements relevant to Health Telematics (e.g. data transmission, digital signature, electronic address and envelope etc.) and redefine some established legal concepts such as document, authentication etc. through signature, register etc.
2. changes in law caused by the use and implementation of digital signature technologies in different legal systems

Definitions and Re-definitions of Terms

With the advent of Health Telematics a number of hitherto established processes and legal concepts can be called into question or can be considered no longer appropriate. Innovation in telecommunication technologies has created many new forms of communication and relationships, which may range from direct communication through digitalized means to communication via trusted third parties and automated communication between computers with little or no human intervention. Similarly, the exchange and archiving of documents through digital means raises the questions of whether such documents can be recognised for legal purposes, i.e. is a digitally transferred or archived health care record a medical record in accordance to health legislation and medical law? As for signatures, the same debate is relevant. Except for a number of specific purposes where manuscript signature is specifically stipulated, a signature is usually a means of identification, authentication and agreement. Digital signature and encryption technologies can fulfil these purposes, but it is still uncertain whether that would stand up in court in a legal action.

Transmission

A central element in Health Telematics is transmission of data/documents. In the potentially volatile environment of digital transmission a number of new issues are raised in relation to matters such as if and when a message has been transmitted, if and when it has been received, if and when it has been accessed and/or corrupted by third parties. A special difficulty is raised by the fact of transborder data flow and obstacles due to differing national legislation.

During the workshop, the following proposals have been made in relation to some of these questions. The principle rule is that messages are transmitted in an appropriate way. The point of time when a message is sent can be determined as the time when the information system is given the appropriate instructions and when these have been acknowledged by the system. A message can be regarded as received when it arrives at the receiver's electronic address, which can be an information system, a mail box provided by a third party etc.

According to the experts at the workshop, the main elements of the process of transmission are: electronic address, electronic envelope, linked purpose to documents, open networks versus close networks, standardisation versus legislation, transborder data flow. The workshop participants recommended to define these terms. Further, they advanced a definition for 'electronic place', which was described as an abstract location that exists only in a virtual world to describe a starting or finishing point to the transmission of data (e.g. mailbox) and is not comparable to a concrete location in the real world.

Documents

Paper Documents

A paper document consists of three aspects:

1. the carrier (the sheet of paper)
2. text and pictures (the physical representation of the information)
3. information about the originator to verify the authenticity (usually a written signature).

These aspects are often seen as material/physical. The connections among carrier, text and signature are self-evident. Therefore, normally only the carrier is mentioned. It provides parameters and structure to one finalised representation of the content. These aspects are physically „locked“ via the paper that carries the information in one „unchangeable“ and durable combination.

Paper documents are in principle unique physical examples, originals. Every paper document to a certain degree contains a unique physical character as an object, often given by the written signature. A paper document may as a physical example be in a person’s possession, thereby establishing legal rights. The paper is the physical carrier of a certain right.

In a paper document the stored state and the readable state are identical. The paper document is immediately readable and the storing is normally in a language that the user will understand without special training. Consequently a manipulation of a paper document has to be a material attack, traceable upon the physical object. An individual often makes a visual authenticity control when he is reading an important paper document.

Digital Documents

A digital document is defined as an electronic document with a digital signature or a digital stamp. A digital signature can be described as the result of a transformation of an electronic record by means of a unique key, making it possible to establish if the content originates from the source designated as the issuer. A digital stamp is the result of a transformation of an electronic record by means of a unique key making it possible to establish if the content originates from the legal person or authority designated as the issuer.

Digitally represented information from a traditional point of view may not be described as a physical object. Electronic documents confer new dimensions. Descriptions of electronic documents will normally make immaterial wordings, not physical objects, the starting point.

There is no lock for the information in an electronic document without certain technical authentication procedures. The fixed and „locked" state in a paper document is replaced by the possibility to process the data into a variety of constellations (potential documents). Data are not unique as physical examples. The unique existence of IT-material is built upon the storing and transmission of original contents. An IT stored record has no other unique character than those bound to the pattern of digits.

The function of paper as carrier of a legal right is normally not possible to recreate in the IT environment where, for example, a data transmission results in the multiplying of the digital bits and not the physical transference of a physical example. The legal functions built into a certain physical object are, in the IT-environment, normally substituted by registration in a database.

In a digital document the stored state and the readable state are not identical. The documents must be transformed to a recognisable format for human scrutiny. A manipulation of a digital record consists of untraceable alterations of a bit pattern which may be manipulated during the transferral among different states and media. The visual authenticity control of a paper document has no correspondence in the IT-area and it is not possible to make use of the routines elaborated to inspect manipulations of paper documents.

Registers

The term register in every day language may be used in related but clearly different meanings. One aspect focuses on the fact that a register creates some order in a set of objects that may or may not be part of the register. Even if the term register is sometimes used just to describe a data storage space, the more interesting register concept from a legal point of view is clearly something more.

In contrast to a document, a register is not just data. Irrespective of it being a traditional paper based system or a computerised register the register has certain functional characteristics. The three main functions of a register are

1. to store records
2. to retrieve and deliver records (excerpts of the register)
3. to protect the register against unauthorised use (integrity and confidentiality).

The paper based register system should, for the analogy to be complete, be regarded as the combination of the physical records and files and the human being operating the register.

A key element of a register is also that some entity is responsible for the register, the contents, the availability of the service offered and often it is ensured by outside regulations that a register is unique in it's domain. While the content of a document is usually associated with a physical person as the issuer, a register usually has a legal person (a company or government organisation) as the responsible entity. The responsibility of a register is tied to the correct functioning of the system, making it possible to generate the constellation of information needed for the moment based on excerpts of the complete register.

Public Key Certificate

A public key certificate (PK-certificate) is used to establish a subject's identity (either that of a person of a system) by means of a designated public key. The certificate is issued by a certification authority (CA) within the scope of a certain security policy. The certificate is digitally signed by using the private key of the issuing CA. Hence the signature of the certificate need not be protected against forgery, and the certificate may be distributed via insecure channels and stored in any certificate system.

The public key certified with a certificate will be used in one of the following three types of applications:

- digital signature applications;
- authentication applications;
- key encipherment applications.

The merging strategy

Merging or separation of certificates

The authentic connection between a distinguished name and a public key and the authenticity of the connection between a distinguished name, the format used in the net-world to identify a user, and a professional status of a health professional can be provided in different ways. Since these are different issues, especially with regard to the various responsibilities involved in each, they can be handled separately. Please note that in this case the distinguished name is the link between the public key and the professional status. In other words, there is no possibility of assigning a public key to a wrong professional status and vice versa.

On the other hand, however, it is also possible to merge these issues (only from an external point of view) mainly by adding the professional status as an identification component to the distinguished name. In this case, information about the professional status may be submitted from a certain professional authority e. g. the physicians chamber to a TTP in charge with of authentication of the connection between the distinguished name and the public key.

In the following some key aspects of both strategies are discussed regarding their advantages and disadvantages.

Responsibilities

Following the merging strategy, the revocation of the professional status (general authorisation) may lead to the automatic revocation of the public key and vice versa. With regard to this aspect, the question whether health care professional cards should be open to other sectors may be a key factor of choice. It is noteworthy that the authentication of identity is a matter common to all sectors. Thus, revocation conditions for public keys determined in a general inter-operable policy may completely differ from those for professional status determined in the specific policies of the respective professional authorities.

To be up-to-date for the professional status is another problem which the merging strategy faces. Especially, with regard to revocation lists delivered intern by the respective professional authority to the collaborating TTP, the following question has to be answered: Where is the board of responsibilities for the problems caused by possible delays? It has to be borne in mind that the collaborating TTP is the one who actually operates with the world outside.

Functioning

Following the merging strategy, the professional authority has to comply to the TTP, at least from an external point of view, i.e. the user's view. One is obviously forced to operate with the „either-or-principle“ according to the possible technical means.

The merging strategy does not provide any means by which one can respect the different validity periods needed for the public key and the professional status. For instance, if certificates are used and the professional status has changed, this change cannot be taken into account unless the corresponding certificate is reissued. Please note that a public key may remain secure for 5 years, but the professional status can change more frequently (new professions, special qualifications, etc.).

Technical complexities

From an external point of view, the merging strategy provides a simple method for making the information needed available: The whole „package“ is made available at once. The problem is that at any time of verification, automatically the authentication of both public key and the professional status is verified which is not necessary in many cases.

The separation strategy

Responsibilities

Following the separation strategy, the problem of revocation does basically not occur. Moreover, revocation conditions for the public key and the professional status can be defined and realised independently. In contrast to the merging strategy, there is no need for checking the consistency of the information available on each side following the separation strategy.

Precise procedures for dealing with respective revocation lists can be developed and controlled. It is noteworthy that controllability is a key factor for a TTP in order to survive.

Functioning

The separation strategy provides the possibility for the realisation of different structures (hierarchies) for the respective professional authorities and the TTP (e.g. ID-CA) in charge of the authentic connection between the distinguished name and the public key.

Professional authorities may operate at least on a regional level. TTPs however, can and maybe should operate in a more distributed way (e.g. several CA-levels).

Technical complexities

The separation strategy provides a choice for the technical means to be used by the respective authorities for providing authenticity. For instance, it may be the best way to use X.509 certificates for the public key but other types of certificates or even authentication servers for the professional status. At the latest when certificates are used, the separation strategy requires obviously more storage place as the merging strategy.

Following the separation strategy, the demand for making information available may grow on the side of the professional authority. On the other hand, however, the TTP does not have to provide information about the professional status any more, which is a decrease in his demand. Nevertheless, users are dependent on more than one information source when using the separation strategy.

The disadvantage of the separation strategy is that whenever the authentication of both identity and professional status is required, the verification becomes more complicated, mainly because of the extra verification for the professional status. Please not that providing authentic information for both public key and professional status is a matter common to both strategies.

Characteristics of Trusted Third Parties

The main requirement for a TTP especially for a certification authority is to be impartial and independent in order to inspire enough trust first to the users, finally to the court which has to value the electronic document signed with a digital signature. So users should be able to feel confident about the accuracy of the data, for example, that the public key belongs to the person to whom the certificate says it belongs or that the certification authority has not been bribed to issue a certificate or to disclose its private key, and about the accuracy of the public key directory.

In reality there is not much experience with real TTPs: So far national banks and international chambers of commerce have demonstrated their interest to offer such services and some private entities have started providing such services. Although from a technical point of view these entities can provide the security services aforementioned, the two following reasons indicate that a regulation of the legal framework of TTPs would be desirable:

An organisation offering security services under legal requirements would offer more reliability than others without any state regulation. Fulfilling the legal requirements would allow a company /person to obtain a license as a certification authority to offer security services. Licensing establishes a minimal regulatory system to provide a level of reliability in certification authority practises. Moreover, the licensed authority should be subject to control and audit regularly and the results of such controls will authorise the entity to continue his activity or will dis-authorise it.

A legal infrastructure with predictable principles governing the various relationships would provide clarity: the duties and responsibilities of the certification authority would become defined and this would favour the use of the technology. Using national legal structures and not international ones would comply with the principle of subsidiarity and legitimate responsibilities of the states.

Some main characteristics should be fulfilled by every TTP even if no law exists which forces the authorities to do so. The TTPs should offer proper security services. They should act with diligence (reasonable care) in ascertaining the critical facts about the subscriber's identity and the key pair. The entities should not have commercial, financial or political interests. The financial responsibility may be assured through security arrangements such as surety bonds or standby letters of credit, or perhaps through liability insurance when it becomes available.

The development of TTP services should be developed by the market in an open and competitive environment. The role of TTPs should not be attributed by law to special entities to avoid the creation of monopolies. The users should have the free choice which kind of TTP should be responsible for them. Nevertheless, at first it makes sense that the chambers of physicians in Germany or equal organisations in other European countries act as TTP because health professionals will trust more their own organisation than other bodies.

Changes in Law Caused by Implementation and Use of Digital Signatures

This issue was discussed in relation to the three jurisdictions represented at the workshop, namely Belgium (Yves Poullet, Rosa Julia-Barceló), Germany (Wolfgang Kilian, Zoi Kardasiadou, Marion Herbst), and Sweden (Per Furberg). The general conclusion was that the implementation and use of digital signature technologies will not fundamentally influence the legal systems under discussion. Several minor changes in law will, however, be necessary.

Belgium

In the opinion of the Belgian legal experts Yves Poullet the relationships between the various parties involved in communication will become increasingly important. It is thus essential to create greater clarity and perhaps establish communication models where necessary. Communication should structured in accordance with a finality principle. Legal regulation is one means to achieve this aim. Another is the establishment of legal standards for data transfer.

The digital signature changes parts of the legal world which have used hand-written signature for identification of somebody for the last two centuries. But problems appearing can be facilitated when concentrating on the technical process of signing with the help of a computer. One should have in mind the following four principles when processing medical data:

- decompose the process in the different phases
- sign each element
- keep the trace of the entire places
- sign the final document.

These principle ideas fit with the EU Directive and with Belgian law. If the principles are respected, questions of liability and evidence are clear and privacy problems do not play such an important role.

Germany

For the German legal expert, Wolfgang Kilian the issues of documents, digital documents and registrations should be given much attention. Physicians will increasingly communicate digitally and in view of the fact that medical records come under professional secrecy according to §203 of the German Criminal Law, health care providers must be subject to control. Strict liability will become an increasingly applied legal concept and the remaining risks may be covered by insurance policies. Furthermore, the storage and long term archiving of medical records should improve.

Wolfgang Kilian believes that these technical developments will require further legal regulations in the area of data protection and data security. Existing systems should develop stepwise new models and secure standards.

In Germany, a lot of aspects in the medical sector will change. Probably each medical record will be stored in a database, e.g. lab tests, that is produced for a certain purpose. Diagnoses will be owned by the physicians themselves whereas the patient is the owner of his data. The problem of ownership must be solved. Indirect communication will mainly be the type of changing information. The following laws will be changed in minor aspects:

- civil law because it defines the term document, that is not defined in the Signature Act which is discussing only security mechanisms connected with the use of a digital signature;
- the civil procedure law because of § 416 Civil Procedure Law; moreover the principle of strict proof should be introduced;
- the criminal law, because § 203 German Criminal Law deals with professional secrecy; furthermore faults during the data transfer need to be discussed;
- the Medical Infrastructure Act;
- the Archive Act because it contains regulations for the kind and time of archiving;

- the data protection/security law because so far it only offers technical solutions;
- exchange agreements because they should explain the transfer of data from one database to the other, the format and the point of time when data reach the receiver.

Sweden

The Swedish legal expert Per Furberg believes that is it essential to define the terms document and register. Those definitions must in turn be compared with the relevant laws and regulations and correlation should be mapped out. A description of normal routines will lead to a description of routines in IT. The identification of different legal areas will be the result of the whole process of establishing general principles. Until new and improved models can be put forward, the existing ones should be retained.

Principle ideas of Swedish law are not touched by the introduction of a digital signature. But a few minor changes in the following laws of the authorised legal system are necessary:

- the Legal Administrative Procedure Act because it includes a definition of a document.;
- the Legal Medical Records Act because it demands a signature;
- contract law because it includes a model agreement for business over networks;
- law of partnership and company law;
- archival law because it organises national archives where personal data are long time stored in a so far quite simple way;
- civil procedure law;
- criminal law because it needs definitions for the values being protected and for access rights;
- criminal procedure law;
- parts of the Swedish Constitution.

The General International Context

The legal experts agreed on some points independent of the different countries:

1. A complex data transfer between the patient and the health care provider with different senders exists. This new situation makes it necessary to define a chain of information with a final information at the end (finality principle).

2. Digital communication over networks will grow. But the digital signature as one aspect is no typical network function but one function to increase security during the ways of transmission in networks that still have to be defined. Strict liability can then be one of the consequences.

3. The long time archiving is one of the problems in IT surroundings that must be solved. A new organisation of stored data influencing the data protection laws and a data security law will be discussed in detail.

4. Different legal problems in certain legal areas must be defined, general principles must be found out, new routines in IT surroundings must lead to new models.

SIREN will provide the dissemination of the results found in discussions in the next months. One proposal to do so was made during the workshop: During two or three day seminars in the whole world organised by the regional leaders the results will be distributed.

7.4. Register of Relevant Documents and Websites

ABA - American Bar Association
Section of Science and Technology, Information Security Committee

Document Digital Signature Guideline

See: http://www.abanet.org/scitech/ec/isc/dgs.html.

BESTS - Business Environment Study of Trusted Services
Study in EU INFOSEC Programme, ETS section

Document Final report

See: http://www.bests.org./Results/results.html.

EGE – European Group on Ethics in Science and New Technologies

Document Opinion N. 13: Ethical Issues of Health Care in the Information Society

See: http://europa.eu.int/comm/sg/sgc/ethics/en/opinions.htm

ESSI – European Electronic Signature Standardisation Initiative

Document	Final Report of the ESSI Expert Team

See: http://www.ict.etsi.org/

ETSI - European Telecommunications Standards Institute

Document	Telecommunications Security; Electronic signature standardisation report; Draft TR 101 xxx VO.4.2 (1998-11)

See: http://docbox.etsi.org/tech-org/security/open/el-sign/Elec_Sign_standard.doc

European Law

Documents

95/46/EC	Directive on the protection of individuals with regard to the processing of personal data and the free movement of such data
97/66/EC	Directive on the processing of personal data and the protection of privacy in the telecommunication sector
COM(1998)297	EU Directive on Electronic Signatures
COM(1998)585	Green paper on Access to Public Sector Information
92/59/EEC	Directive on the General Product Safety
93/42/EEC	Directive on Medical Devices
COM(1998)586	Draft Directive on Electronic Commerce
95/62/EC	Directive on the application of open network provision to voice telephony
98/10/EC	Directive on the application of open network provision to voice telephony and on universal service for telecommunications in a competitive environment
97/7/EC	Directive on the protection of consumers in respect of distance contracts
21/12/1998	Action Plan Promoting Safer Use of Internet
3381/94 EC	EU Dual-Use of goods regulation (amended by Regulation (EC)

See: http://europa.eu.int/eur-lex/en/index.html

ICC - International Chamber of Commerce

Document GUIDEC - General Usage in International Digitally Ensured Commerce

See: http://www.iccwbo.org/guidec2.html

IMIA - International Medical Informatics Association - Working Group IV

Data Protection in Health Informatics Systems

See: http://hinf.uvic.ca/imia_wg4/, and http://www.imia.org

ISHTAR - Implementing Secure Health Care Telematics Applications in Europe

Project in TAP (Telematics Applications Programme - DG XIII); key project for the management of security issues in health care

Documents Deliverables

See: http://www.echo.lu/search.htm→ TAP 4th FP → ishtar →
http: //ted.see.plym.ac.uk/ishtar/

MEDSEC - Health Care Security and Privacy in the Information Society

Project in ISIS (Information Society Initiatives in Standardisation (DG IIIB)

Documents Final reports

See: http://www.ispo.cec.be/isis/isishome.htm

OECD - Directorate on Science, Technology and Industry

Documents Recommendation of the Council concerning guidelines for cryptography policy and Guidelines for Cryptography Policy, 1997
Ministerial Conference Report: Realising the Potential of Global Electronic Commerce, Ottawa, Oct. 1998
Action Plan for Electronic Commerce

See: http://www.oecd.org/dsti/sti/it/, http://oecd.org/dsti/sti/it/secur/

SEMRIC - Secure Medical Record Information Communication

Project in ISIS (Information Society Initiatives in Standardisation (DG III B)

Documents Final reports

See: http://www.ispo.cec.be/isis/isishome.htm

TESS /SOSENET - Telematics for Social Security/ Social Security Network

Initiative under the IDA programme (DG III, DG V)

Document Reports

See: http://www.ispo.cec.be/ida/text/english/tess1.htm

TrustHealth 1

Trustworthy Health Telematics 1. Project of the Fourth EU Health Telematics Applications Programme, 1997 - 1998. Its results formed the bases of most solutions implemented and published internationally up to 1999.

Deliverables see: http://www.ramit.be/trusthealth

TrustHealth 2

Trustworthy Health Telematics 2. Project of the Fourth EU Health Telematics Applications Programme, 1998 - 2000.

See: http://www.med.uni-magdeburg.de/fme/institue/ibmi/dmi/respo/th2.htm

UNCITRAL - United Nations Commission on International Trade Law
Working Group on Electronic Commerce

Documents	Draft Uniform Rules on Electronic Signatures
	Planning on Future Work on Electronic Commerce: Digital Signatures, Certification Authorities and Related Legal Issues
	Model Law on Electronic Commerce
	Model Law on Legal Aspects of Electronic Interchange (EDI) and Related Means of Communication

See: http://www.un.or.at/uncitral , http://www.mpo.cz/english/ and http://verisign.com/

7.5. Extractions from Relevant Documents

7.5.1 European Electronic Signature Standardisation Initiative (EESSI)

Final Report of the EESSI Expert Team, 20th July 1999

Hans Nilsson, iD2 Technologies, Sweden (Project leader)
Patrick Van Eecke, ICRI-K.U.Leuven, Belgium
Manuel Medina, Univ of Catalunya, Spain
Denis Pinkas, Bull, France
Nick Pope, Security & Standards Consultancy, UK

Executive Summary

The European Commission has proposed to the European Parliament and to the Council a Directive to provide a common framework for electronic signatures. The

Directive covers electronic signatures used for authentication in general as well as a particular type of "qualified" electronic signatures, which have legal equivalence to hand-written signatures. The Directive also identifies requirements that have to be met by service providers supporting electronic signatures and requirements for signers and verifiers. These requirements need to be supported by detailed standards and open specifications which also meet the requirements of European business, so that products and services supporting electronic signatures can be known to provide legally valid signatures – thus furthering the competitiveness of European business in an international market.

Under the auspices of the ICTSB, European industry and standardisation bodies have launched the European Electronic Signature Standardisation Initiative (EESSI). EESSI has the objective of analysing the future needs for standardisation activities in support of the European Directive on electronic signatures in a coherent manner, particularly in the business environment. An expert team appointed by EESSI has produced this report.

It should be understood that this report has been put forward with the intent of proposing standards on the basis of an open implementation framework for electronic signatures including signatures in compliance with the proposed Directive. It is not the intention of this report to establish standards that would be mandatory to support the Directive, but rather identify requirements for standards that would facilitate an open market of products and services that meet the requirements of the directive.

The most important findings of the expert team are summarised as follows:

- International standards adopted and/or developed by industry should avoid the need for detailed regulations as far as possible. A framework relating legislation and standardisation is proposed in this report.
- Standards are urgently needed, and wherever possible, reference to existing recognised international standards should be preferred to the development of new standards. This report has made initial recommendations for the use of existing standards.
- Standardisation requirements can be foreseen in two main areas: qualitative and procedural standards for information security and technical standards for product interoperability.
- In those cases where standards for signature products are recognised as meeting the requirements of the Directive, conformance assessment and certification could be performed by an accredited body under the European EN 45000 accreditation scheme or by a national body using equivalent criteria. A harmonised European scheme and guidelines for conformance assessment of signature products should be developed through the European co-operation for Accreditation (EA). Any standards conformance assessment scheme in this area, and the general conformance scheme against requirements of the Directive need to be aligned.

- A first set of technology-specific components should be defined that can be used to provide a technical framework for qualified electronic signatures, using asymmetric cryptography and certificate based verification, and supported by trustworthy hardware devices such as smart cards. This is needed to provide a common point of reference that is known to meet the requirements of the Directive within the shortest practical time-scale. As the market for electronic signatures develops, standardisation should encompass variations and alternatives to this first set.
- For certification service providers, the following security-related standards are needed:

  - General security management codes of practice, e.g. BS7799 part 1 and part 2.
  - Specification of security requirements for trustworthy systems used by CSPs. For this EESSI recommends that initially specific requirements should be placed on the cryptographic modules being used (e.g. using FIPS 140-1 or equivalent) with more general requirements based on a risk analysis. Also, a suitable protection profile based on the Common Criteria (ISO 15408) may be needed.
  - A baseline Certificate Policy for service providers issuing qualified certificates. EESSI recommends that the policy is written according to the IETF PKIX framework RFC 2527 but should also include references to general security standards as described above.
  - Specification of policy requirements for providers of trusted time-stamping services.

- For signature creation and verification products, the following security-related standards are needed:

  - Specification of security requirements for trustworthy hardware devices used as secure signature creation devices. For this, EESSI recommends concurrent acceptance and usage of FIPS 140-1 (or equivalent standard) and a suitable Protection Profile based on Common Criteria (ISO 15408). Although specification of a security target according to ITSEC also could be possible, the Common Criteria is preferred as it is more recent and has global recognition.
  - Specification for the creation of electronic signatures including recommendations on the user interface.
  - Specification of signature verification products and procedures.

- A number of standardisation activities may be initiated and carried out by various bodies as a result of the proposals in this report. Hence, there is a strong need for technical co-ordination between these activities to ensure that a consistent standardisation framework is developed.
- In the area of interoperability, the following standards are most needed:

  - Technical standard for the syntax and encoding of electronic signatures, supporting multiple signers and role signatures that are verifiable long after their initial use. EESSI recommends that this is based on a profile of and extensions to the CMS standard (RFC 2315, shortly to be replaced).
  - Profiles for PKI operational management protocols based on the Internet PKIX RFCs.
  - Profile for Qualified Certificates based on X.509.

Further details of these work areas, as well as initial proposals as to the best European or international organizations that should execute them, are given in section 8 of this report.

Finally, EESSI also proposes that:

- An " Electronic Signature Standardisation Industry Advisory Group" is established in due course under the auspices of ICTSB, to give recommendations to the Commission's "Electronic Signature Committee". The Advisory Group should be composed of recognised technical experts in the area of electronic signatures from the vendor and user communities.
- An "International Electronic Signature Forum" is arranged, under the auspices of a suitable international organisation, to promote and co-ordinate international activities in the area of electronic signatures.
- Interoperability trials between suppliers of electronic signature products and services should be encouraged to promote the implementation of interoperable solutions.

7.5.2 DIRECTIVE 1999/93/EC

of the European Parliament and of the Council of 13.12.99 on a Community Framework for Electronic Signatures

<u>**ANNEX I**</u>

Requirements for qualified certificates

Qualified certificates must contain:

(a) an indication that the certificate is issued as a qualified certificate;

(b) the identification of the certification-service-provider and the State in which it is established;

(c) the name of the signatory or a pseudonym, which shall be identified as such;

(d) provision for a specific attribute of the signatory to be included if relevant, depending on the purpose for which the certificate is intended;

(e) signature-verification data which correspond to signature-creation data under the control of the signatory;

(f) an indication of the beginning and end of the period of validity of the certificate;

(g) the identity code of the certificate;

(h) the advanced electronic signature of the certification-service-provider issuing it;

(i) limitations on the scope of use of the certificate, if applicable; and

(j) limits on the value of transactions for which the certificate can be used, if applicable.

ANNEX II

Requirements for certification-service-providers issuing qualified certificates

Certification-service-providers must:

(a) demonstrate the reliability necessary for providing certification services;

(b) ensure the operation of a prompt and secure directory and a secure and immediate revocation service;

(c) ensure that the date and time when a certificate is issued or revoked can be determined precisely;

(d) verify, by appropriate means in accordance with national law, the identity and, if applicable, any specific attributes of the person to which a qualified certificate is issued;

(e) employ personnel who possess the expert knowledge, experience, and qualifications necessary for the services provided, in particular competence at managerial level, expertise in electronic signature technology and familiarity with proper security procedures; they must also apply administrative and management procedures which are adequate and correspond to recognised standards;

(f) use trustworthy systems and products which are protected against modification and ensure the technical and cryptographic security of the processes supported by them;

(g) take measures against forgery of certificates, and, in cases where the certification-service-provider generates signature-creation data, guarantee confidentiality during the process of generating such data;

(h) maintain sufficient financial resources to operate in conformity with the requirements laid down in the Directive, in particular to bear the risk of liability for damages, for example, by obtaining appropriate insurance;

(i) record all relevant information concerning a qualified certificate for an appropriate period of time, in particular for the purpose of providing evidence of certification for the purposes of legal proceedings. Such recording may be done electronically;

(j) not store or copy signature-creation data of the person to whom the certification-service-provider provided key management services;

(k) before entering into a contractual relationship with a person seeking a certificate to support his electronic signature, inform that person by a durable means of communication of the precise terms and conditions regarding the use of the certificate, including any limitations on its use, the existence of a voluntary accreditation scheme and procedures for complaints and dispute settlement. Such information, which may be transmitted electronically, must be in writing and in readily understandable language. Relevant parts of this information must also be made available on request to third-parties relying on the certificate;

(l) use trustworthy systems to store certificates in a verifiable form so that:

- only authorised persons can make entries and changes,
- information can be checked for authenticity,
- certificates are publicly available for retrieval in only those cases for which the certificate-holder's consent has been obtained, and
- any technical changes compromising these security requirements are apparent to the operator.

ANNEX III

Requirements for secure signature-creation devices

1. Secure-signature-creation devices must, by appropriate technical and procedural means, ensure at the least that:

(a) the signature-creation-data used for signature generation can practically occur only once, and that their secrecy is reasonably assured;

(b) the signature creation data used for signature generation cannot, with reasonable assurance, be derived and the signature is protected against forgery using currently available technology;

(c) the signature-creation-data used for signature generation can be reliably protected by the legitimate signatory against the use of others.

2. Secure signature creation devices must not alter the data to be signed or prevent such data from being presented to the signatory prior to the signature process.

ANNEX IV

Recommendations for secure signature verification

During the signature-verification process it should be ensured with reasonable certainty that:

(a) the data used for verifying the signature correspond to the data displayed to the verifier;

(b) the signature is reliably verified and the result of that verification is correctly displayed;

(c) the verifier can, as necessary, reliably establish the contents of the signed data;

(d) the authenticity and validity of the certificate required at the time of signature verification are reliably verified;

(e) the result of verification and the signatory's identity are correctly displayed;

(f) the use of a pseudonym is clearly indicated; and

(g) any security-relevant changes can be detected.

7.6. Relevant Bodies and Institutions

Legal instruments having an impact on Health Telematics are often originating from institutions or supra-national bodies. A selection of those are described here in short. Furthermore, a number of bodies stimulating the legal and technical discussion are listed.

ABA - American Bar Association

The Section on Science and Technology of the ABA was created in 1997. Since then members with diverse backgrounds in areas such as computer law, engineering, physics and medicine work through five substantive divisions and twenty-four committees to explore the legal implications raised by new technical and scientific discoveries and developments. The Section's divisions are: Administrations Division, Computer Law Division, Communications Law Division, Electronic Commerce (EC) Division, and Life Sciences and Physical Sciences Division. The last one has installed committees on Health Care Informatics and Medical Practice / Medical Research.

The Section provides a forum for members to explore new and emerging topics such as electronic commerce and digital signatures, online payment mechanisms such as smart cards and digital cash, scientific misconduct, law and the internet, multimedia and interactive technology, information security and privacy, telecommunication law, and many more. The Section publishes a quarterly bulletin which contains a substantive article on each issue, as well as the Jurimetrics Journal which contains articles regarding the issues surrounding law, science, medicine, and technology. The Information Security Committee of the EC Division has produced a legal overview of the use of cryptology, electronic signatures and entity authentication over an open network, called the Digital Signature Guideline.

For further information on ABA and its Section of Science and Technology: http://www.abanet.org/scitech/home.html

CEN

The mission of the European Committee for Standardisation (CEN) is to promote voluntary technical harmonisation in Europe in conjunction with world-wide bodies and its partners in Europe. In Europe, CEN works in partnership with CENELEC - the European Committee for Electrotechnical Standardisation and ETSI - the European Telecommunications Standards Institute. CEN has an agreement for technical co-operation with ISO, the International Organisation for Standardisation, and has signed the World Trade Organisation (WTO) Code of Good Practice for the preparation, adoption and application of standards.

National Members of CEN are the European national standards bodies which have the duty of sending balanced delegations to the policy-making bodies and technical committees. Furthermore, organisations representing broad European interests may become associate members. Industry and other social partner have seats in the various policy-making committees. European federations can apply for liaison status with individual committees. Standards organisations from Central and Eastern Europe are affiliated to CEN.

CEN is governed by the General Assembly of its National Members which is responsible for the budget, membership, and appointment of officers. The Administrative Board is the authorised agent of the Assembly to direct CEN's operation.Responsible to the Board is a Management Committee. This committee enforces the decisions taken by the Administrative Board and Technical Board and ensures the operational management of CEN. The Technical Board controls the standards programme and promotes its execution by the Management Centre, technical committees and other bodies. The CEN Management Centre in Brussels provides the focal point for the co-ordination and management of the organisation and its processes.

CEN Technical Committees (CEN/TCs) are responsible for the programming and planning of the technical work, for the monitoring and the execution of the work, and for the management of the standards making process, including the respect of CEN's policies and the consensus building amongst all interested parties represented through the CEN national members, the CEN associates and the affiliates.

Once the need for a European standard has been firmly established, and non-duplication of work verified (CEN may also use an international standard), a team of experts is set up in the framework of a CEN/TC.

Of the numerous Technical Committees operating within CEN, eight have work programmes in the ICT (Information and Communication Technologies) sector. CEN has placed these ICT-related TCs under its ISSS (Information Society Standardisation System) umbrella. Here only two of the CEN/ISSS Technical Committees shall be mentioned:

CEN/TC 224 Machine readable cards, related device interfaces and operations

CEN/TC 251 Health informatics.

Formal adoption of European standards is decided by a weighted majority vote of all CEN National Members and is binding on all of them, i.e. compulsory national implementation of European standards and withdrawal of conflicting national standards.

For further information see: http://www.cenorm/be ; http://www.cenorm/be/isss/ http://www.centc251.org/

EC - European Commission

A number of bodies have been active in regard to digital signature and other legal issues which are the target of this study:

DG XIII/7 - Senior Officials Group - Information System Security (SOG-IS)'s activity on digital signature: Council Decision 92/242/EEC of 31.3.1992 "Security of Information Systems" defined the necessity for a SOG-IS to advise the Commission. To support the implementation of the action lines described in the Decision, and the work of SOG-IS, a programme comprising a number of studies and investigations was launched in 1992: "INFOSEC '92. A follow-up set of projects was implemented building on the results of the earlier projects and assessing various security considerations in areas including telecommunications, "trusted services", etc.

DG XIII/7 - INFOSEC and ETS Programmes activity on digital signature and TTPs: Within the INFOSEC Programme, a number of projects on TTP concepts and issues have been carried out. Some of them (e.g. BOLERO, EBRIDGE, TESTFIT and THIS) are relevant to digital signature as they have aimed to establish system concepts and service practices to support the use of digital signature for business applications.

Calls for tender were published in 1996 and 1997 on "Preparatory work concerning the development of a Europe-wide network of TTP services (ETS)" that under the Task "Legal services" addressed digital signature. The reports resulting from this work as well as from another study on standardisation issues for the ETS are available on the INFOSEC Web page. A further Call for tender was published in 1997 addressing the "development of a technical and a legal Framework for trust for security products, systems and services (e.g. digital signature)".

DG XV E/5 activity on digital signature: In order to provide the Commission with an "overview of national policies, EU policies, existing and envisaged rules and regulations, as well as (de facto) practice including export controls, concerning digital signatures in the Member States as well as in the EU's main trading partners" a study was finally launched at the beginning of 1997 and has been completed recently.

DG III B/6 - Interchange of Data between Administrations (IDA) Programme's activity on digital signature: IDA has just finished its second phase (1994-1998). Its projects have deal with security issues, in particularly issues of cryptography, including encryption, digital signatures and the use of smart cards.

Besides these, the European Commission undertook a number of initiatives: The first Commission statements and policy elements for the use of encryption and digital signature in the framework of the Electronic Commerce have been defined in the Communication to the Council and the Parliament titled "A European Initiative in Electronic Commerce" - COM(97)157 dated April 16, 1997. On October 8, 1997, the Commission adopted the Communication to the European Parliament, the Council, the Economic and Social Committee and the Committee of the Regions "Ensuring security and trust in electronic communication: Towards a European Framework for Digital Signatures and Encryption" On May 13, 1998, a proposal for a directive establishing a legal framework for the use of electronic signatures was put forward by the European Commission: "Proposal for a European Parliament and Council Directive on a Common Framework for Electronic Signatures" (COM(97) 503. COM(1998) 297 final)

For further information see: http://www.cordis.lu/home.htm, http://www.cordis.lu/src/ets.htm, and http://www.ispo.cec.be/ida/

EESSI -The European Electronic Signature Standardisation Initiative

Several standards initiatives have been launched at the national, regional and international level by organisations and industry. Activities have been undertaken by e.g. the International Chamber of Commerce (ICC), the World Wide Web Consortium (W3C), and the ABA (American Bar Association). However, it was felt that these were not sufficient to respond to the legal requirements, and that a consistent and coherent approach is necessary. Industry and European standardisation bodies have been requested by the European Commission to analyse in a coherent manner, the future needs for standardisation activities in support of essential minimum legal requirements as stated in the Directive on Electronic Signatures. In order to identify gaps and the need for additional standards, specifications, agreements, workshops or other form of consensus building, an assessment of the actual situation should be undertaken.

To meet the requirements of the Commission, the EESSI was launched under the direction of a steering group composed of industry representatives, representatives of standardisation bodies, EC observers, and experts in the field. The Steering Group is assisted in its work by the expert team, which will work to meet the ESSI objectives, i.e. to prepare the grounds to support the emerging legal framework for electronic signatures in the EU. Based on the legal requirements set by the Directive, standardisation efforts should be oriented towards use of electronic signature and such products, certification schemes and services for the end-user.

For further information see: http://www.ict.etsi.org/

EGE - European Group on Ethics in Science and New Technologies

The European Group on Ethics in Science and New Technologies (EGE), inaugurated in February 1998. is convened by the European Commission. This group succeeds the group of advisors on ethical implications of biotechnology (1991-1997). The Secretariat-General of the Commission, acting in close co-operation with the Group's chairperson, is responsible for organising the work of the Group, and its secretariat.

EGE is an independent, multi-cultural and multi-disciplinary group of experts, appointed by the European Commission. The Group's 12 members represent a variety of different viewpoints and disciplines. On the basis of the principles laid down in the European Treaties (which make reference to the fundamental rights defined by the European Convention of Human Rights of the Council of Europe), the EGE endeavours to draw up common rules to enable the internal market to operate in accordance with Europe's ethical values.

As an independent consultative Committee within the European Union, the European Commission may request opinions from the Group, but also the European Parliament and Council of Ministers. Parliament has asked to have a direct contact with the Group, at a time when the general public are increasingly interested in the ethical aspects of science and technology.

In July 1999, the EGE adopted for the first time an opinion on the ethical aspects of the Information Society. The EGE believes that now is the time to put in place measures to protect personal health data. Consideration of the ethics of health care in society is necessary, it says, as there has been an explosion of the use of information and communications technologies in health care, marking the beginning of a wide range of uses of personal health data.

Personal health data are the most sensitive data about an individual, says the group: 'They not only focus on an individual's medical history, but also behavioural patterns and possibly sexual life'. Because this data can be used for a number of purposes outside of the health care sector, (such as social security, containment of medical expenditure, statistics and research and insurance, amongst others) the EGE says citizens are entitled to legal protection from abuse of this data resource. Essentially, it says, it is a human right that personal data should be held confidential.

The EGE will now suggest that a directive on medical data protection be established within the framework of the existing Data Protection Directive, to address the issues arising from the use of personal health data, and that a European Patient's Charter be adopted to cover the main principles of 'infoethics' in the health care sector.

For further information see:
http://europa.eu.int/comm/sg/sgc/ethics/en/opinions.html.

EHTEL – European Health Telematics Association

EHTEL started in December 1998 as a feasibility study funded for two years by the European Commission, DG XIII. The purpose of this feasibility study was "to assess levels of interest in organising a forum which would bring together all the European actors concerned with the development of the use of telematic solutions in health care, i.e. health care authorities, health care providers, information technology industry, telecommunication operators, pharmaceutical laboratories, publishers, providers of content..."

In September 1999, the consortium invited representatives of those actors to a launch meeting in Erlangen (Germany), in order to validate the findings and discuss priorities. 104 delegates from 21 nationalities and institutions represented 18 countries and the different categories of actors.

At the end of 1999, the EHTEL association was founded as a neutral, non-profit association of health care actors for the promotion of telematics solutions in health care across Europe.

The objectives of this initiative are to "deliver service functions to the key groups of actors in the European health sector, to facilitate transparency, exchange, and collaboration, and to achieve efficient valuable use of telematics in the health sector.

The EHTEL organisation consists in a Board of Directors and an Executive Committee. Up to now, 56 institutions and 18 individuals have applied for membership. Work is done in a number of working groups which are concentrating on topics relevant for a certain group of actors (e.g. health insurers) or on horizontal themes like e-health or electronic patient record.

For further information see: http://www.ehtel.org

ETSI - European Telecommunications Standards Institute

The ETSI is a non-profit organisation whose mission is to determine and produce the telecommunications standards. It is an open forum that unites 696 members from 50 countries, representing administrations, network operators, manufacturers, service providers, and users. ETSI produces voluntary standards - some of these may go on to be adopted by the EC as the technical base for Directives or Regulations. ETSI's Work Programme is based on, and co-ordinated with, the activities of international standardisation bodies.

ETSI consists of a General Assembly, a Board, a Technical Organisation and a Secretariat. The Technical Organisation produces and approves technical standards. It encompasses ETSI Projects (EPs), Technical Committees (TCs) and Special Committees. More than 3.500 experts are at present working for ETSI in over 200 groups.

The central Secretariat of ETSI comprises about 100 staff members. In order to promote and accelerate standardisation, additional experts work on a full time basis at the ETSI Headquarters. At present, there are about 30 Specialist Task Forces with around 100 experts. Up to now, over 2800 ETSI deliverables have been published.

The ETSI Technical Committee Security is responsible for ES standardisation within ETSI. The TTP ad hoc Working Group of TC SEC is in charge to execute the programme. The final draft of the ETSI Standard is scheduled for TC SEC approval in September '99.

Four aspects of electronic signatures have been selected for standardisation in order to meet minimum interoperability requirements for electronic business transactions. More information is to be found in "ES Mission Statement" and about background of the work in "ETSI Report, Electronic Signature Standardisation". ETSI has established an open discussion area on electronic signatures. Reports and working drafts are available from the open file server.

For further information see: http://www.etsi.org/
and http://www.etsi.org/sec/el-sign.htm

ICC -International Chamber of Commerce

The ICC was founded in 1919 as a non-governmental organisation of more than 7.000 companies and business associations in more than 140 countries. ICC national committees present ICC views to their governments and alert the Paris headquarters to national business concerns. One of ICC's main activities is harmonisation of trade practices. ICC commissions made of business experts meet regularly to formulate recommendations on a broad range of issues affecting commerce, investment and business practice. ICC has fourteen commissions, of which two shall be named here. The Commission on Intellectual and Industrial Property acts at the international level in favour of appropriate protection of such properties as patents, trademarks and copyrights, and new technologies, i.e. biotechnology, software, digital technology. Therefore one of its current priorities is to examine intellectual property issues raised by the development of digital technology and information infrastructures.

ICC's Commission on Telecommunications and Information Technologies is co-operating with the European Commission on continued liberalisation of markets for telecommunications services and with the Council of Europe Committee of Experts on Data Protection. It also works together with WTO and the International Organisation of Standardisation (ISO). With OECD and other intergovernmental authorities ICC co-operates in regard to cryptography policy guidelines.

ICC's Information Security Working Party together with ICC commissions and other parties had drafted guidelines for uniform international authentication and certification practices (called GUIDEC) within the ICC Electronic Commerce Project.

For further information see: http://www.iccwbo.org/

IMIA - International Medical Informatics Association Working Group IV

In the same way that the International Medical Informatics Association (IMIA) grew out of Technical Committee 4 (TC4) of the International Federation for Information Processing (IFIP), the Working Group IV – Data Protection in Health Information Systems – grew out of WG 2 of TC4 which was formed in the early 1970s. This early WG arranged a working conference in 1979 and in May 1979, when TC4 was transformed into IMIA. Out of this conference the first WG4 monograph resulted which addressed all issues of privacy, confidentiality, data protection, and data security. During this period the Council of Europe developed its Convention 108. The second monograph appeared in 1983, after this the focus of attention changed a little bit as a number of countries their national data protection activities. The work continued with the foundation of the corresponding WG of the European Federation for Medical Informatics, IMIA's regional group for Europe. Workshops were organised and held at IMIA and EFMI conferences, and other occasions. Co-operation with the European Commission was set up when the Commission developed its programme AIM-Advanced Informatics in Medicine, in the context of which a Working Conference was held.

As the field developed further, activities and contacts with national and international bodies were intensified (e.g. INFOSEC programme of the European Commission, Standardisation Organisations CEN, EWOS, and ISO). The list of topics discussed at conferences and workshops was enlarged, e.g. to legal issues in data protection and training, management, and development of the security culture.

For further information see IMIA Yearbooks, and web-sites: http://www.imia.org, http://hinf.uvic.ca/imia_wg4/

ITU- International Telecommunications Union

The International Telecommunications Union (ITU) became a specialised agency of the United Nations in 1947. ITU is an intergovernmental organisation, within which the public and private sectors co-operate for the development of telecommunications. ITU adopts international regulations and treaties governing all terrestrial and space uses of the frequency spectrum as well as the use of the geostationary-satellite orbit, within which countries adopt their national legislation. It also develops standards to facilitate the interconnection of telecommunication systems on a world-wide scale regardless of the type of technology used. The ITU fosters specifically the development of telecommunications in developing countries.

188 States are member of ITU; is has around 400 members. These are scientific and industrial companies, public and private operators, broadcasters, and regional/international organisations.

The supreme organ of the ITU is the Plenipotentiary Conference, composed of representatives of all the members. It sets out general policy. The ITU Council, composed of 46 members, has to consider broad telecommunication policy issues in order to ensure that the Union's policies and strategy respond to the constantly changing telecommunication environment. The ITU structure comprises three sectors, namely: (1) The Radiocommunication Sector, (2) The Telecommunication Standardisation Sector (ITU-T); and (3) The Telecommunication Development Sector.

The ITU-T is the international body for fostering co-operative standards for telecommunications equipment and systems. Telecommunications Standardisation Conferences (held every four years) approve, modify or reject draft standards called Recommendations because of their voluntary character, and approve the programme of work. Standardisation work is carried out by 14 Study Groups in which representatives of the ITU-T membership develop Recommendations for the various fields of international telecommunications. ITU works closely with all standards organisations.

For further information see: http://www.itu.int/

ISO – International Organisation for Standardisation

The International Organisation for Standardisation (ISO) is a world-wide federation of national standards bodies from some 130 countries, one from each country. ISO is a non-governmental organisation established in 1947. The mission of ISO is to promote the development of standardisation and related activities in the world with a view to facilitating the international exchange of goods and services, and to developing co-operation in the spheres of intellectual, scientific, technological and economic activity.

The technical work of ISO is highly decentralised, carried out in a hierarchy of some 2.850 technical committees, subcommittees and working groups. In these committees, qualified representatives of industry, research institutes, government authorities, consumer bodies, and international organisations from all over the world work together. Some 30.000 experts participate in meetings each year.

The major responsibility for administrating a standards committee is accepted by one of the national standards bodies that make up the ISO. The Central Secretariat in Geneva acts to ensure the flow of documentation in all directions, to clarify technical points with secretariats and chairmen, and to ensure that the agreements approved by the technical committees are edited, printed, submitted as draft International Standards to ISO member bodies for voting, and published. To date, ISO's work has resulted in some 12.000 international standards.

The scope of ISO is not limited to any particular branch; it covers all technical fields except electrical and electronic engineering, which is the responsibility of the International

Electrotechnical Commission (IEC). The work in the field of information technology is carried out by a joint ISO/IEC technical committee (JTC 1).

ISO and the IEC co-operate on a joint basis with the ITU (International Telecommunication Union). Like ISO, the IEC is a non-governmental body, while the ITU is part of the United Nations Organisation and its members are governments. The three organisations have a strong collaboration on standardisation in the fields of information technology and telecommunications.

For further information see: http:www.iso.ch/

LAB of European Commission DG XIII

The European Commission, Directorate XIII (Information Market Policy) has set up a Legal Advisory Board which deals with a variety of activities centred around legal issues of the information market. This Board consist of about 60 experts from all European Member States.

These experts are coming from law faculties of universities, research institutions, ministries, and law firms. According to the broad spectrum of the information market, these aspects represent the whole range of techno-legal issues: From data protection and privacy to IPR law, from telecommunications law to computer crime and security. Only a few describe their areas of special interest to be Health Telematics.

The Legal Advisory Board has set up a web-site where the bi-monthly LABnews are published. This contains information on new developments regarding the most important legal issues in the EU, USA, Japan, and some other countries. From this web-site documents in English, German, Spanish, French, and Italian can be downloaded. Furthermore, results of the meetings of the Board are to be found there.

For further information see: http://www.echo.lu/legal/en/news

OECD – Organisation for Economic Co-operation and Development

The Organisation for Economic Co-operation and Development unites 29 member countries in an organisation. It provides governments a forum for discussion and development of economic and social policies. Experiences are compared, common problems discussed, and work to co-ordinate domestic and international policies is undertaken. These exchanges may lead to agreements to act in a formal way.

Information exchanges between OECD governments are provided by a Secretariat. Parts of this Secretariat collect data, monitor trends, analyse and forecast economic developments. Others undertake research on social changes or evolving patterns in trade, technology, and more. This work is supporting discussions by member countries meeting in specialised committees of the OECD. These specialised committees review progress in defined areas - there are about 200 committees, working groups and expert groups.

The staff of the OECD Secretariat in Paris, organised in a dozen directorates, works directly or indirectly to support the activities of the committees. In the context of this study the most important ones are: Science, Technology and Industry; Trade, and Electronic Commerce.

The Working Party of the Trade Committee is a very specific body of OECD, preparing "the work of the Trade Committee, looking in particular at the more technical aspects of issues". The promotion of trade liberalisation has been always central to OECD although it has not been used to conduct formal international negotiations on trade – which is the role of the World Trade Organisation (WTO, see there). But OECD is complementing the work of the WTO. "Leaving effective trade negotiations to WTO, the OECD develops a long-term vision of the development of international trade relations".

For further information see OECD homepage: http://www.oecd.org

WA - WASSENAAR Arrangement

The Wassenaar Arrangement (WA) is the first global multilateral arrangement on expert controls for conventional weapons and sensitive dual-use goods and technologies. It was approved by 33 co-founding countries in July 1996 and began operations in September 1996. The participating states seek through their national policy to ensure that that transfer of arms and dual-use goods and technologies do not contribute to developments that undermine international and regional security and stability. The WA countries maintain effective export control s for the items on the agree lists which are reviewed periodically to take into account technological developments and experiences gained. WA members are required to report arms transfers as well as transfers or denials of transfers of certain controlled dual-use items.

Participating states meet on a regular basis in Vienna, where the Arrangement has established its headquarter and a small secretariat. Decisions are made by consensus.

The Participating States of the Wassenaar Arrangement are: Argentina, Australia, Austria, Belgium, Bulgaria, Canada, the Czech Republic, Denmark, Finland, France, Germany, Greece, Hungary, Ireland, Italy, Japan, Luxembourg, the Netherlands, New Zealand, Norway, Poland, Portugal, the Republic of Korea, Romania, the Russian Federation, the Slovak Republic, Spain, Sweden, Switzerland, Turkey, Ukraine, the United Kingdom, and the United States.

For further information see: http://www.wassenaar.org/

WHO - World Health Organisation

The objective of WHO is "the attainment by all peoples of the highest possible level of health". In support of this objective the Organisation has a wide range of functions, including to promote technical co-operation and promotion of standards. WHO recognised that advances in information and communication technologies could offer opportunities for global health improvement. It therefore convened an international Group Consultation at the end of 1997, "in order to advise it on the development of a Health Telematics policy and on the examination of both the benefits and risks of the use of these technologies, and propose action for integration of Health Telematics in the overall policy and strategy for the attainment of health for all in the 21st century." An Advisory Board on Health Telematics has been established.

For further information see: http://www.who.int/ism-htp/Telematics/policy.htm

WIPO - World Intellectual Property Organisation

The World Intellectual Property Organisation (WIPO), founded in Stockholm in 1967, is an intergovernmental organisation with headquarters in Geneva, Switzerland. It is one of the 16 specialised agencies of the United Nations system of organisations. WIPO is responsible for the promotion of the protection of intellectual property throughout the world through co-operation among States, and for the administration of various multilateral treaties dealing with the legal and administrative aspects of intellectual property. There are two main branches, namely, industrial property, which chiefly means inventions, trademarks, industrial designs and appellations of origin; and copyright, which chiefly means literary, musical, artistic, photographic and audio-visual works

The number of States members of WIPO was over 170 in August, 1998, in addition, six States were party to treaties administered by WIPO but had not yet become members of WIPO. A number of bilateral, regional and multilateral conventions, treaties, and agreements in the intellectual property field (industrial property and copyright and neighbouring rights) have been achieved by WIPO.

For further information see: http://wipo.org/eng/main.html

WTO - World Trade Organisation

The World Trade Organisation is the "only international organisation dealing with the global rules of trade between nations." It is the successor of the GATT organisation. The WTO has more than 130 members, more than 30 are negotiating membership. Decisions are made by consensus and by the entire membership. The WTO's agreements have been ratified in all member's parliaments.

The Ministerial Conference is the top-level decision making body of WTO. Below this is the General Council consisting of ambassadors and delegation heads from the member countries. Goods Council, Service Council and Intellectual Property (TRIPS) Council report to the General Council. Numerous specialised committees, working groups and working parties deal with individual agreements and specific areas like interaction between trade and competition policy. In 1998, the Ministerial Conference decided that WTO should also study the area of electronic commerce. The WTO Secretariat, based in Geneva, is headed by a Director-General. The Secretariat's main duties are to supply technical support for the various councils and committees and the Ministerial Conferences, to provide technical assistance for developing countries, to analyse world trade, and present WTO affairs to the public and media.

For further information see WTO homepage: http://www.wto.org

W3C - World Wide Web Consortium

The W3C was founded in 1994 with the goal to lead the World Wide Web to its full potential by developing common protocols that promote its evolution and ensure its interoperability. W3C is an international industry consortium, jointly hosted by the Massachusetts Institute of Technology Laboratory for Computer Science, the Institute National de Recherché en Informatique et en Automatique, and the Keio University Shonan Fujisawa Campus. Services provided by the Consortium include: a repository of information about the World Wide Web for developers and users; reference code implementations to embody and promote standards; and various prototype and sample applications to demonstrate use of new technology. Initially, the W3C was established in collaboration with CERN, with support from DARPA (U.S. Defense Advanced Research Project Agency) and the European Commission. Today, more than 300 institutional members are working on various topics, e.g. in interest groups on electronic commerce and web security. Personal privacy issues, intellectual property rights, trust management, encryption

Computer system security, network security, trust management and authentication services, message validation, personal privacy issues, and cryptography as well as intellectual property rights are discussed. Results are published in technical documents, specifications and recommendations in journals and on the web.

For further information see: http://w3c.org

7.7. Literature and Material for further Studies

Grey Literature:

B. Barber, K. Louwerse, J. Davey, White Paper on Health Information Security, Implementing Secure Health Care Telematics Applications in Europe (ISHTAR Deliverable No. 37). NHS Executive's Information Management Centre, Leeds, 1997.

F. Beuting, R. Baumgart, C. Stark, Evaluation und Zertifizierung eines Health Professional Card-Systems. TÜV Informationstechnik GmbH, Essen, 1997.

Department of Health, UK, Using electronic patient records in hospitals - legal requirements and good practice, NHS Executive, Health Service Circular 1998/153. London, 1998.

Deutscher Bundestag, 13. Wahlperiode, Vierter Zwischenbericht zum Thema „Sicherheit und Schutz im Netz“ der Enquête-Kommission: Zukunft der Medien in Wissenschaft und Gesellschaft - Deutschlands Weg in die Informationsgesellschaft. Bonn, 1998.

S. Erber-Faller, Stellungnahme zur EU-Richtlinie Elektronische Signatur. Bundesnotarkammer, Cologne, 1998.

F. M. Ferrara, Authorisation and Security in the HISA Standard Middleware-based Health Care Information Systems Architecture and in the DHE Middleware, GESI - Gestione Sistemi per l'Informatica srl & Consorzio EDITH, DOC GE-205 version 1.0. Rome, 1998.

F. Fisher, The patient's view of confidentiality, in: Conference Proceedings Current Perspectives in Health Care Computing Conference Part II, Harrogate 17-19 March 1997, The British Computer Society Health Informatics Specialist Groups (eds.), BJHC Ltd., Weybridge, 1997.

S. Hadjerrouit, Rechtsverträgliche Gestaltung medizinischer Expertensysteme im Krankenhaus, Dissertationsschrift. Berlin, 1993.

B. Hornung, H. Farroukh, European Potential and Security Aspects of Health Care Professional Cards - Technology Assessment Study 2. Philipps-University Marburg (Deliverable of the EUROCARDS Concerted Action), 1995.

Interdisciplinary Centre for Law and Information Technology, The Legal Aspects of Digital Signatures, Study for the European Commission, DG XV, ICRI. Kath. Universiteit, Leuven, 1998.

R. Julia-Barceló, Th.C. Vinjel, Another Step Towards a European Framework for Electronic Signatures: The Commission's Directive Proposal. CRID, Namur, 1998.

G. Klein (ed.), Case Studies of Security Problems and their Solutions. SIREN Deliverable 3.1, Stockholm, 1999.

W.W. Lowrance, Privacy and Health Research, A Report to the U.S. Secretary of Health and Human Services, Washington, 1997.

H. Mensch, A. van der Werff, R. Menke, Security Problems and Solutions of Regional Health Information Networks for Europe RHINE - Initiative, Requirements, Technology, Security, Contribution to SIREN, 1998.

Ministerium für Wissenschaft, Forschung und Kunst Baden-Württemberg: Beweisrechtliche Sicherheit digitaler Krankenakten, hier: Zivilprozessuale Bewertung, MWFK, Referat III, Internes Papier, Stuttgart, 1997.

O. Rienhoff, U. Piccolo, M. Herbst, P. Wenzlaff, The Identification of Health Professionals in Respect to Health Professional Cards. University of Göttingen, Physicians Chamber of Lower-Saxony, Hannover, 1998.

S. Schulz, O. Rienhoff, B. Lutterbeck, The digital image as evidence (under the German Law), Proceedings of CAR 97. International Symposium on Computer and Communication Systems for Image Guided Diagnostics and Therapy 1997. Elsevier, Amsterdam, 1997, pp. 685-689.

B. Stanberry, Working Group on Legal and Policy Issues, in: Telemedicine in the 21st Century: Opportunities for Citizens, Society and Industry - Workshop Proceedings. European Commission (ed.), 1999, pp. 79 - 85.

A. B. Suleiman, Malaysia's Telemedicine Flagship Application, Presentation at 9th World Congress on Medical Informatics
Medinfo '98. Seoul, 1998.

TELEMED '98 - Telematik im Gesundheitswesen - Tagungsband zur 3. Fortbildungsveranstaltung und Arbeitstagung, G. Steyer, M. Engelhorn, W. Fabricius, K.-P. Löhr, T. Tolxdorff, (eds.). FU Berlin, Berlin, 1998.

Teletrust Deutschland e. V., Kryptoreport - Kryptographische Verfahren im Gesundheits- und Sozialwesen in Deutschland, Arbeitsgruppe 3: Medizinische Anwendungen einer vertrauenswürdigen Informationstechnik. Erfurt, 1998.

O. Ulrich, „Protection Profile“ - ein industriepolitischer Ansatz zur Förderung des “neuen Datenschutzes”. Graue Reihe (17), Europäische Akademie zur Erforschung von Folgen wissenschaftlich-technischer Entwicklungen (ed.), Bad Neuenahr-Ahrweiler, 1999.

World Health Organisation/DGO/98.1, A Health Telematics Policy, Report of the WHO Group Consultation on Health Telematics. Geneva, 1997.

Books:

R. Anderson (ed.), Personal Medical Information. Security, Engineering, and Ethics, Personal Information Workshop, Cambridge, UK, 1996, Proceedings. Springer-Verlag, Berlin, 1997.

H. Bäumler, (ed.), Der neue Datenschutz, Datenschutz in der Informationsgesellschaft von morgen. Luchterhand, Neuwied, 1998.

B. Barber, A. Treacher, K. Louwerse, (eds.), Towards Security in Medical Telematics - Legal and Technical Aspects. Studies in Health Technology and Informatics, Vol. 27. IOS Press, Amsterdam, 1996.

J. Berleur, K. Brunnstein (eds.), Ethics of Computing: Codes, Spaces for Discussion and Law, A handbook pepared by the IFIPS Ethics Taste Group. Chapman & Hall, London 1997.

B. Blobel, (ed.), Datenschutz in medizinischen Informationssystemen. DuD Fachbeiträge, Vol. 23. Vieweg, Braunschweig, 1995.

G. Brenner, W. van Eimeren, C. Sachse, K.H. Vöge, (eds.), Telematik-Anwendungen im Gesundheitswesen - Nutzungsfelder, Verbesserungspotentiale und Handlungsempfehlungen - Schlußbericht der Arbeitsgruppe 7 des Forum Info 2000. Schriftenreihe des Bundesministeriums für Gesundheit, FORUM INFO 2000 Bonn. Vol. 105. Nomos Verlagsgesellschaft, Baden-Baden, 1998.

J. Dumortier, P. van Eecke, The Legal Aspects of Digital Signatures. Interdisciplinary Centre for Law and Information Technology, European Commission (eds.), Mys & Breesch, Gent, 1998.

A. Glade, H. Reimer, B. Struif, (eds.), Digitale Signatur & Sicherheitssensitive Anwendungen. DuD Fachbeiträge. Vieweg, Wiesbaden, 1995.

R. Hamm, K.P. Möller (eds.), Datenschutz und Forschung, Forum Datenschutz, Band 7. Nomos Verlagsgesellschaft, Baden-Baden, 1999.

P. Iwansky, Datenschutzrechtliche Probleme von Chipkarten am Beispiel der geplanten Patientenkarte unter besonderer Berücksichtigung der europäischen Entwicklung, Mensch & Buch Verlag, Berlin, 1999.

M. Nerlich, R. Kretschmer, (eds.), The Impact of Telemedicine on Health Care Management. Studies in Health Technology and Informatics, Vol. 64. IOS Press, Amsterdam, 1999.

J. Roberts, P. Wilson, (eds.), Navigating the legal waters - Report on the HC98 Satellite Session supported by the European Commission. Conference Proceedings, Current Perspectives in Health Care Computing 1998, Part 11, Harrogate 23-25 March, Health Informatics Committee of the British Computer Society (ed.), Cromwell Press, Trowbridge, 1998.

R. Rogers, J. Reardon, Barriers Arising from Legal Accountability and Ownership, in: Barriers to a Global Information Society for Health - Recommendations for International Action - Report from the project G8-Enable. Studies in Health Technology and Informatics, Vol. 63. IOS Press, Amsterdam, 1999, pp. 19 - 20.

E. und S. Schach, W. Kilian, A. Podlech, B. Schlink, C. Schönberger, Daten für die Forschung im Gesundheitswesen - Statistische und rechtliche Klärung ihrer Weitergabe. Beiträge zur juristischen Informatik, H. Brinckmann, W. Kilian (eds.). Vol. 20, S. Toeche-Mittler-Verlag, Darmstadt, 1995.

SEISMED Consortium (ed.), Data Security for Health Care - Volume I: Management Guidelines. Studies in Health Technology and Informatics, Vol. 31. IOS Press, Amsterdam, 1996.

B. Stanberry, (ed.), The Legal and Ethical Aspects of Telemedicine, The Royal Society of Medicine Press Ltd, London, 1998.

URLs:

G. Buonomo, Italian Laws and Regulations Concerning the Creation, Storage, and Transmission of Documents by Means of Computer-Based Systems and Digital Signature, OECD-EMEF Workshop on Cryptography Policy Paris, France, 1997.
http://www.oecd.org/dsti/sti/it/secur/act/emefdocs.html

H. Burggasser, W. Dorda, J. Gambal, G. Gell, H. Ingruber, W. Kotschy, E. Leitgeb, J. Mittheisz, K. Pfeiffer, O. Pjeta, M. Pregartbauer, H. Tinhofer, Rahmenbedingungen für ein logisches österreichisches Gesundheitsdatennetz "MAGDA-LENA", Version 14.3, STRING-Kommission des BMAGS, Wien, 1999.
http://akh-wien.ac.at/STRING/MAGDA-LENA.html

Enquête-Kommission "Zukunft der Medien in Wirtschaft und Gesellschaft - Deutschlands Weg in die Informationsgesellschaft" Vierter Zwischenbericht zum Thema Sicherheit und Schutz im Netz. Deutscher Bundestag, 1995.
http://bundestag.de/ftp/9000500a.html

EUROMED - European Trust Structure, ETS Consortium. Information Society Standardisation Programme.
http://euromed.iccs.ntua.gr/

European Commission, DG XIII, Communication from the Commission to the European Parliament, the Council, the Economic and Social Committee and the Committee of the Regions Ensuring Security and Trust in Electronic Communication: Towards a European Framework for Digital Signatures and Encryption, Document COM(97)503.
http://www.ispo.cec.be/eif/policy/97503toc.html.

IMIA- The International Medical Informatics Association, WG IV "Data Protection".
http://www.imia.org

ISHTAR Consortium, Implementation of Secure Health Telematics Applications in Europe. Project of the Fourth EU Health Telematics Applications Programme.
http://www.etho.be/projects/ishtar/

Koops, B.-J., *Crypto Law Survey,* Version 14.3, Feb. 1999.
http://cwis.kub.nl/~frw/people/koops/lawsurvey.html.

Ministry of Research and Information Technology, The Copenhagen Hearing, European Expert Hearing on Digital Signatures and Encryption, April 23-24, 1998.
http://www.fsk.dk/fsk/div/hearing/first.html.

OECD Cryptography Policy Guidelines
http://www.oecd.org/dsti/iccp/crypto_e.html.

OECD Guidelines for the Security of Information Systems
http://www.oecd.org/dsti/iccp/legal/secur-en.html.

OECD Guidelines on the Protection of Privacy and Transborder Flows of Personal Data
http://www.oecd.org/dsti/iccp/legal/priv-en.html.

Remotti, L., Legal and Regulatory Issues Concerning the TTPs and Digital Signatures - Final Report, INFOSEC - ETS, European Commission, DG XIII-07. 1998.
http://www.cordis.lu/infosec/src/stud2fr.html.

Schadow, G., Tucker M., Rishel W., Secure HL7 Transactions using Internet Mail (draft-ietf-ediint-hl7). Internet Draft (EDIINT Working Group), July 21, 1998.
http://www.ietf.org/internet -drafts

A. Servida (ed.), Digital Signature - Inventory of International Regulatory, Standardisation and Commercial Activities, Version 3.3, Sept. 1998
http://www.ispo.cec.be/ecommerce/didisign/htm

Swedish Interministerial Working Group on Digital Signatures, Digital Signatures - A Technological and Legal Overview, Ministry of Transport and Communications, Stockholm, Sweden, 1998.
http://www.regeringen.se/info_rosenbad/departement/kommunikation/ds98_14/

Teletrust Deutschland e.V., Arbeitsgruppe 3 "Medizinische Anwendungen einer vertrauenswürdigen Informationstechnik" (ed.), Kryptographische Verfahren im Gesundheits- und Sozialwesen.
http://www.teletrust.de/wf/K_R2/inhalt.html.

The Caldicott-Committee, Report on the Review of Patient-identifiable Information, National Health Service Information Authority,
December 1997.
http://www.nhsia.nhs.uk/imt4nhs/general/caldico/caldico1.html.

S. van der Hof, Digital Signature Law Survey, Version 3.4, May 1999.
http://cwis.kub.nl/~frw/people/hof/DS-lawsu.html.

P. Veiga, D. Domingos, National Security Regulations and the Use of Cryptography for Trans-border Communication, Project: ICE-TEL - Interworking Public Key Certification Infrastructure for Europe, Del. 3, 1997.
http://www.di.fc.ul.pt/investigaco/projectos/ia

Journal Articles:

F.-A., Allaert, The Use of Health Information for Controlling the Costs of Delivering Health Care: Does the End Justify the Means? International Journal of Bio-Medical Computing, 1996 (43): pp. 72-82.

B. Baeriswyl, Patientendaten: Ware im Gesundheitsmarkt? Datenschutz und Datensicherheit, 1998.22 (7): pp. 403-406.

A. R. Bakker, B. Barber, K. Ishikawa, K. Yamamoto, Common Security Solutions for Communicating Patient Data - Proceedings of IMIA Working Group 4 Working Conference November 22-25 1997 International Journal of Medical Informatics (Special Issue), 1998 (1).

E. Deutsch, Die Beweiskraft der EDV-Dokumentation bei zahnärztlicher Behandlung. MedR, 1998 (5).

Deutscher Ärztetag, 101., Entschließung: Patientenschutz und moderne Kommunikationstechniken. Deutsches Ärzteblatt 95, Heft 23, 1998 (51): p. 1179.

Health Care Information Management & Communications (Official Journal of Canada's Health Informatics Association), Vol. XII, No. 4, 1998.

J. F. Hoppe, Telemedizin und internationale Arzthaftung. MedR, 1998 (10): pp. 462-468.

K. R. Iversen, T. O. Grotan, Socio-technical Aspects of the Use of Health-related Personal Information for Management and Research. International Journal of Bio-Medical Computing, 1996 (43): pp. 83-91.

B. Kane, D. Z. Sands, (for the AMIA Internet Working Group), Guidelines for the Clinical Use of Electronic Mail with Patients. Journal of the American Medical Informatics Association, 1998.5 (1 Jan/Feb).

E.-H. W. Kluge, Professional Ethics as Basis for Legal Control of Health Care Information. International Journal of Bio-Medical Computing, 1996 (43): pp. 33-37.

E.-H. W. Kluge, Fostering a Security Culture: a Model Code of Ethics for Health Information Professionals. International Journal of Medical Informatics, 1998 (49): pp. 105-110.

F. Leiner, Internationale Förderung und Trends in der Telemedizin. Das Krankenhaus, 1998 (8): pp. 469-473.

F. Malamateniou, G. Vassilacopoulos, P. Tsanakas, A Workflow-Based Approach to Virtual Patient Record Security. IEEE Transactions on Information Technology in Biomedicine, Special Issue on Emerging Health Telematics Applications in Europe. Part I, Sept. 1998, Vol. 2, No. 3, pp. 139-145.

C. Pick, D. Zarn, Security "Best Practices" for Health Care. Health Care Information Management & Communications (Official Journal of Canada's Health Informatics Association), 1999.XIII (2): pp. 57-60.

A. Rossnagel, Die Sicherheitsvermutung des Signaturgesetzes. NJW, Heft 45, 1998, pp.3312-3320.

W. Schorre, Starke Kryptographieverfahren unverzichtbar. Deutsches Ärzteblatt / Praxis Computer, 1998 (2): pp. 2-4.

B. Stanberry, The Legal and Ethical Aspects of Telemedicine. 1: Confidentialityand the Patient's Rights of Access. Journal of Telemedicine and Telecare, 1997.3 (4): pp. 179-187.

B. Stanberry, The Legal and Ethical Aspects of Telemedicine. 2: Data Protection, Security and European Law. Journal of Telemedicine and Telecare, 1998.4 (1): pp. 18-24.

J. P. van Gigch, The Potential Demise of OR / MS: Consequences of Neglecting Epistemology. European Journal of Operational Research, 1989 (42): pp. 268-278.

G. Weck, Key Recovery - Möglichkeiten und Risiken. Informatik-Spektrum, 1998.21 : pp. 147-158.

H.-E. Wichmann, Epidemiologie und Datenschutz - Wege zur partnerschaftlichen Zusammenarbeit. Informatik, Biometrie und Epidemiologie in Medizin und Biologie 1999 (30): pp. 35-44.

B. Woodward, The Computer-Based Patient Record and Confidentiality. The New England Journal of Medicine, Vol. 333, 1995, No. 21, pp. 1419-1422

Index of Subjects and Names